SOCIAL
HIERARCHIES

SOCIAL HIERARCHIES

Essays Toward a
Sociophysiological
Perspective

EDITED BY
Patricia R. Barchas

Contributions in Sociology, Number 47

 GREENWOOD PRESS
Westport, Connecticut
London, England

Library of Congress Cataloging in Publication Data

Main entry under title:

Social hierarchies.

  (Contributions in sociology, ISSN 0084-9278 ; no. 47)
  Bibliography: p.
  Includes indexes.
  1. Sociobiology—Addresses, essays, lectures.
2. Social interaction—Addresses, essays, lectures.
3. Dominance (Psychology)—Addresses, essays, lectures.
4. Small groups—Addresses, essays, lectures.
I. Barchas, Patricia R. II. Series.
HM106.S723   1984   304.5   83-22600
ISBN 0-313-23165-6 (lib. bdg.)

Library of Congress Catalog Card Number: 83-22600
ISBN: 0-313-23165-6
ISSN: 0084-9278

First published in 1984

Greenwood Press
A division of Congressional Information Service, Inc.
88 Post Road West
Westport, Connecticut 06881

Printed in the United States of America

10 9 8 7 6 5 4 3 2 1

Contents

Figures

Tables

Preface

Emphasizing questions arising from similarities of hierarchical forms of social organization observed across species, these essays use selected animal as well as human models to inquire into the sociophysiological dynamics which underly hierarchical behavior. Hierarchical relational systems are used throughout as prototypes of structural interconnections through which social order may be achieved in small groups. In order to explore hierarchies as a generic form of primate social organization in small groups, these essays proceed from an evolutionary contextual frame, through chapters which illuminate the regularities of hierarchical structures to the last chapters which implicate the brain's attentional system as a chief mediator between an individual's position in the group structure and behavior.

The volume begins with a review of the treatment of biological parameters of human behavior, provided by Drs. Susan Bolin and Robert Bolin. Their evaluation leads them to conclude that focus on the human microorder of social behavior is the proper focus of such inquiry. They agree with the position that a bio-logical basis will be found in association with general rules of human behavior and not in specific actions. In this volume we assume that hierarchies are such general rules that generate be-havior and that there will be discernable sociophysiological mech-anisms associated with them.

The speed, stability and degree of differentiation as hierarchical structures are formed in ad hoc triadic groups of rhesus and college freshmen are compared by Drs. Patricia Barchas and Hamit Fisek. At the level of analysis used, the data suggest it is appro-priate to think of the orders of the two species of primate as having similar form and as representing similar distributions of acts across group members.

Asking the question, "why should species so diverse as animals are from one another, and as all animals are from humans, form dominance hierarchies so similar in structure," Dr. Ivan Chase critically rejects theories that have been proposed by both animal behaviorists and social scientists. To account for the dynamics of hierarchy formation in small groups, he puts forth and tests a new processual model which rests on the interaction process per se, rather than upon individual characteristics. The model implies "a certain lawfulness in the formation of linear structures of in-teraction that can explain the configurations of social relation-ships." He demonstrates that "lawfulness" by testing his model with observations of triads of chickens, a species for which lin-earity or near linearity of structure frequently has been claimed.

In order to determine whether the processes of emergence for-mally delineated by Chase can be detected in a species of primate, Drs. Patricia Barchas and Sally Mendoza analyze data from newly formed triads of rhesus macaques that meet the conditions of Chase's model. The basic formulation does hold in this specie of primate, strengthening the idea that some of the most funda-mental behavioral mechanisms for development of hierarchical relations may be independent of animal type.

Moving on from hierarchy formation, Dr. Henry Walker's chapter concerns the hierarchical pattern in stable groups, after relations have emerged amongst group members. He generates a graph theoretic model out of an exchange theory of human power and influence and tests it on extant data from animal groups to predict dominance rank. In doing so, Dr. Walker moves from dyadic interaction to a characterization of whole group relations and thereby points a way past a methodological stumbling block that has effectively reinforced misconceptions about the locus of group properties being the individual rather than relationships.

In both the emergent and stable phases of hierarchical structures, the degree of regularity of form and process across species increases confidence that there should be associated sociophysiological mechanisms. As an exploratory investigation into this issue, Drs. Suzanne Haber and Patricia Barchas pharmacologically alter the physiology of rhesus monkeys living in groups with developed stable and known hierarchical relationships. They administer low doses of amphetamine, a drug which reliably produces a known core of physiological and psychological effects, and observe the subsequent behaviors amongst group members. While some drug behaviors of target animals are idiosyncratic to the individual, others are determined by their social relationships, including their rank in the hierarchical structure. The study shows differential response to the drug based on relationships determined by position in the hierarchy; the behavioral effects of amphetamine are known to occur at least in part through its effect on the central nervous system's attentional system. Therefore, it is reasonable to ask whether attentional mechanisms are normally involved in the way hierarchies govern behavior.

The final essay develops the notion that attentional processes may be involved in hierarchical regulation of behavior. The authors posit that social hierarchies organize perception of the environment. They suggest that self's perceived postion in such hierarchies helps to specify those social elements of information most likely to be relevant and to which attention should be directed. The chapter reports a limited test of this general hypothesis by using electrophysiological techniques within an established experimental paradigm which holds task constant. Persons manipulated into a high status relative to another increase measures of attention, as predicted. The results strengthen the probability that in small human groups regulation of attention may be a sociophysiological mechanism which tends to assure the mutually coordinated and complementary behavior engendered by social structures such as hierarchies.

Acknowledgments

Thanks are due to those many colleagues and students who have supported and encouraged the development of a social science which draws on biology and neuroscience as well as social psychology, primatology, and sociology. Especially appreciated is the steady support given for this line of interdisciplinary work by Stanford colleagues from the Departments of Sociology, Psychology, Psychiatry and Behavioral Sciences and the Neurosciences. Students from both the social and biological sciences are always generous—if not diplomatic— in sharing their analytic and integrative perceptions of the subject matter. Along with their revitalizing good humor and enthusiasm, they also exhibit a galvanizing impatience for these areas of inquiry to move ahead. That impatience, while shared, must be tempered with the realization that every effort should be made to encourage rigor as the scientific base is developed for the long latent field of sociophysiology.

The volume has benefited from early discussions with Dr. Sally

P. Mendoza. Dr. Paul Colomy, Kinga Perlaki and Valerie Mon-
toya have also contributed to its development. The Harry Frank
Guggenheim Foundation provided early encouragement of this
approach, and gratitude is also felt toward the Office of Naval
Research, represented by Dr. Donald Woodward. The efforts of
Dr. James Sabin, Margaret Brezicki, Maureen Melino, Barbara
Melino, Susan Baker and others of the Editorial Administration
at Greenwood Press in bringing this volume to publication are
appreciated. In particular, Dr. Sabin has been both creative and
helpful. And, Sue Poage has provided reliable and excellent help
throughout the preparation of the manuscript for the publisher.

SOCIAL
HIERARCHIES

1

Sociobiology and Sociology: Issues in Applicability

Robert Bolin and Susan Bolton Bolin

Concern over the possible biological parameters of human behavior is an emerging focus of interest for some sociologists and biologists. With such concern has come dispute and controversy based both on ideological and substantive grounds. Much of the controversy is centered on assertions that sociobiology is a resurrected form of biological determinism at best, or at worst, a new social Darwinism. Others doubt the suitability of a sociobiological approach due to a belief in the radical discontinuity between Homo sapiens and lower primates. This essay will address the issues of the applicability of sociobiological principles in sociology.

In order to examine this issue, we will first review the relationships between the disciplines of ethology, sociobiology and sociology. The controversies over Wilson's (1975) and Van den Berghe's (1974; 1975a) work will be examined along with the popular "ethologizing" (Callan, 1970) of Lorenz (1966), Ardrey (1966) and Morris (1967). We will analyze the critiques of sociobiology and specify what we feel to be the legitimate domain of socio-biology in sociology. The issues which a human sociobiology should address will be likewise presented.

ETHOLOGY, SOCIOBIOLOGY AND SOCIOLOGY

The earliest studies of animal behavior were anecdotal, anthropomorphic and nonsystematic in character. They gave way in Europe at the turn of the century to the pioneering work of zoologists such as Whitman, Heinroth, Huxley and Verweg (Lorenz, 1950). With scientific attentions focused on animal behavior, concern shifted to issues of the causation, adaptation and evolution of behaviors (Tinbergen, 1951). The work of Lorenz and Tinbergen led ethology into its modern phase with a formidable elaboration of theories, methods, and conceptual analyses. Ethology during the 1950's and 1960's built up an important empirical data base; a base that constitutes an important foundation from which contemporary sociobiology has arisen.

The emergence of sociobiology appears to have been facilitated, at least in part, by two factors in biology. While ethologists focused considerable attention on the evolution and evolutionary significance of species-specific behaviors, they never adequately integrated synthetic evolutionary theory with the study of behavior (Alexander, 1975; Mayr, 1963). Further, during the last two decades biologists began using populations not only as a unit of evolutionary change, but as a unit of natural selection as well. The notion of population selection lacked explanatory power and inhibited the incorporation of principles of individual selection in explaining the origins of behavior (Alexander, 1975).

Williams (1966) refuted the notion of population selection and instead argued that natural selection operated at the level of the individual organism or at the level of parents and offspring. While Williams' work was initially controversial, it substantially redirected the research emphasis of biologists working in this area (Alexander, 1975). The notion of natural selection at the level of the individual has become a key element in sociobiological theory. Thus, both the failure of ethologists to adequately utilize evolutionary theory in terms of genetic fitness and the redirection of natural selection theory in biology have been key factors in the growth of modern sociobiology.

Basic concepts used in sociobiology such as behavioral genetics, behavioral ecology and synthetic evolution have been addressed to some degree for decades (Scott, 1950; Herrick, 1956; Hinde and Tinbergen, 1958; Alland, 1967; Wallace, 1973). However, it was Wilson (1971, 1975) who pulled together the disparate threads of sociobiology into a unified if preliminary body of theory. It was the publication of Wilson's *Sociobiology: The New Synthesis* that precipitated the current controversy over the use of sociobiological theory insofar as it applies to Homo sapiens.

As a discipline, sociology has had, at best, an unhappy relationship with biology, particularly with Darwinian evolutionary theory and its variants. The uncritical appropriation of evolutionary principles and their application to societal development by Spencer (for example, Gould, 1977a) has had the unfortunate result of equating evolution with progress both in the popular press as well as among certain academic writers (cf. Quadagno, 1979). The impact of social Darwinist thought on everything from the justification of colonial expansion to U.S. immigration policies is readily apparent. In addition, the misuse of Darwinian theory became a major factor in justifying the continued subordination of women in Western societies (Rossi, 1978).

Due to the excesses of social Darwinism in sociology, sociology swung to its current social-cultural determinist stance, choosing to ignore the human organism almost entirely (Rossi, 1978; Van den Berghe, 1980). Parsons et al. (1953) did allow a theoretical edifice for the "biological organism" as the adaptive subsystem of the general action system, but failed to elaborate on that functional sector in later delineations. Similarly, Parsons (1966) resurrected a form of Spencerian evolutionism and coupled that with his functional paradigm to explain the evolution of societies.

Due to these frequently erroneous and sometimes injurious applications of biological theories, sociologists have made little recent use of biology. Perhaps the first notable call for sociologists to reconsider the human as an animal with a complex history of organic and behavioral evolution came from Van den Berghe (1974). Van den Berghe's article in the *American Sociological Review* was controversial and began a debate over biosocial perspectives in the social sciences, one that has intensified. The subsequent publication of an introductory level text by Van den Berghe (1975a) and its recently published updating (1978) are further reinforcement of his central position in the debate.

THE CONTROVERSY

Public and professional sensitivities to the issues raised by Wilson (1975) and Van den Berghe (1974) were heightened by earlier publication of a number of popular books (Ardrey, 1966; Lorenz, 1966; Morris, 1967; Tiger and Fox, 1971). These books are characterized by "ethologizing" (Callan, 1970), or the simplified application of ethological terms to humans without concern for applicability or homology. With the combined popular writings of Lorenz and Ardrey we have inherited the unfortunate insistence on the "natural" aggressiveness of Homo sapiens and the erroneous linking of territoriality and aggression. Authors have since tried to remove this "ideological overburden" in the study of human territoriality (Suttles, 1972) but it is an idea that endures. The incautious and extravagant analogizing of Morris has created further misinformation as has Tiger and Fox's emphasis on male bonding. All these works are typified by the "naive redescription of human behavior in ethological language" (Callan, 1970:52).

Emblematic of these books' lack of scientific credibility, they have engendered more popular than academic controversy. The same cannot be said for Wilson's (1975) work. Although his Chapter 27, titled "Man: From Sociobiology to Sociology," is but a brief speculative end to a major theoretical and substantive synthesis, it has become the focus of controversy. The dispute between Wilson's human sociobiology and the positions of some sociologists is both substantive and ideological. The emotional component of the latter has clouded over substantive matters to the point where they are frequently ignored.

In an attack on human sociobiology spanning the substantive and ideological, the Science for the People group at Harvard (Allen et al., 1976) have portrayed sociobiology as a new biological determinism and have attempted to refute Wilson's analysis of Homo sapiens. Wilson (1976), in turn, has rebutted their critique of his analysis and accused them of academic "vigilantism." The emotional scope of the debate was highlighted by a water-throwing attack on Wilson by protesters at the American Association for the Advancement of Science meetings (*Science*, 1978).

The publication of Van den Berghe's "Beasts" article, while not provoking the vitriolic attacks endured by Wilson, did produce a number of criticisms. Fischer (1975) accused Van den Berghe of erroneously linking territoriality and aggression, while Moberg (1975) refers to the article as "pithecomorphizing" human behavior. Mazur's (1975) critique on the need to consider levels of social organization when engaging in cross-species comparisons is perhaps the most fruitful and serious of the objections.

More recently the debate has flourished in the *American Sociologist*. Ellis (1977), in an article referring to the decline and fall of sociology, suggested that sociobiology would emerge as sociology's successor. This produced a quick refutation from Eckberg (1977), who accused Ellis of scientism, reductionism and teleology, among other things. In the same issue were a number of letters offering critiques on both sides (*American Sociologist*, November 1977).

In sum, most of the objections to both Wilson and Van den Berghe revolve around issues of determinism, reductionism and, more importantly, applicability. We will address these issues in an effort to justify the application of sociobiological principles to humans. An outline of some major methodological considerations for its application will be presented.

THE SOCIAL SCIENCE CRITIQUE OF SOCIOBIOLOGY

The major sociological objections to sociobiology encompass several charges: it is tautological; it is biologically deterministic; it has moved away from the spirit of Darwinian natural selection; it does not adequately predict patterns of human society; humans are unique as culture-bearing animals and not subject to biogenetic influences on behavior.

The charge that sociobiology is tautological (Sahlins, 1976; Quadagno, 1979; cf. Bolin and Bolin, 1980) has been leveled against all Darwinian evolutionary theory (that is, survival of the fittest means that those who survive are fit). To save the general formulation from being circular, a criterion of success independent of survival must be identified (Gould, 1976). The same holds true for sociobiology's theorem that organisms act in such a way as to maximize inclusive fitness (Barash, 1977). Darwin used fitness to refer to an organism being well adapted in a phenotypic sense. Any trait that aided an organism in its survival increased its fitness (Mayr, 1976). Sociobiologists use fitness in a more specific sense than Darwin's early formulation. Geneticists Wright, Haldane and Fisher redefined fitness to refer to the contribution an individual makes to the gene pool. Inclusive fitness refers to an individual's contribution to the genetic stock directly through its own reproduction and through the reproduction of kin which share genes with that individual. Fitness is thus "a value free algebraic parameter that measures the contribution made by heredity determinants to the differential reproductive rate of organisms" (Stent, 1978:213).

Fitness of an organism must be considered in relationship to changing environments. "Certain morphological, physiological, and behavioral traits should be superior *a priori* as designs for living in these new environments" (Gould, 1976:26). Survival is an expression of superior, or more fit, design. Thus, the independent criterion of fitness is "improved design" of the organism in regard to the demands of a local environment (Gould, 1976). The tautology is only apparent and results from careless formulations of Darwinian principles, not an intrinsic flaw in evolutionary or sociobiological theory.

The charge of determinism (Gould, 1977a) is based on an oversimplified polarization, one that has been the hallmark of the nature-nurture dispute for decades. Gould characterizes sociobiology as arguing for human traits being rigidly predetermined by genetic inheritance. If all sociobiologists argued this, characterizing them as determinists would be accurate. Sociobiology, in fact, speaks to the complex interplay of learning with biological predispositions and potentials (Rossi, 1978; Daly and Wilson, 1978; Barash, 1977; Van den Berghe, 1980), rather than to rigidly determined behavioral traits.

The charge that sociobiology has violated the spirit of Darwinian formulations (Quadagno, 1979; Sahlins, 1976) may be considered on two levels. The most obvious response is that one hundred years of biological research has provided evolutionists with information on the genetic mechanisms underlying evolution, mechanisms that Darwin had no direct knowledge of. In that sense evolutionary theory, including sociobiology, has moved away from Darwin's earliest formulation.

On a second level, the charge made by Sahlins (1976) and echoed by Quadagno (1979) is that sociobiology emphasizes a principle of maximization rather than Darwin's emphasis on "minimum" advantages in differential reproduction. The charge maintains that while Darwin stressed the minimum significant difference in differential reproduction needed to confer selective advantage to individuals, sociobiologists instead stress the maximization of inclusive fitness. This is asserted to reflect the ideological juncture of sociobiology with a more general late capitalist economic metaphor (Sahlins, 1976). In a semantic sense, Sahlins' charge is founded and the more appropriate term would be the "optimization" rather than the maximization of fitness. However, if one examines the contextual meaning of maximization, it is not used in the economic sense of a maximized or ideal strategy (cf. Sahlins, 1976). Rather, maximization of inclusive fitness refers to an individual achieving an advantage in differential reproduction, and in that sense it is consistent with Darwin. Maximization refers to a relative and not absolute reproductive advantage of individual organisms over conspecifics.

Sahlins has also charged sociobiology with failing to predict specific kinship patterns among humans. Sahlins' (1976) argument is based on the incidence of unilineal descent systems and fictive kinship, neither of which, it is argued, is consistent with the notion that individuals should favor those kin who share the greatest percentage of genes. (See Van den Berghe [1980] for an alternative explanation.) Sahlins' critique appears to be simply setting up sociobiology as a straw man. Scientific sociobiology should not attempt to predict the specific localized cultural forms of the human kinship system. Few specific examples of human kinship have a 100 percent correspondence with expected relationships based on shared genetic heritage. However, when looked at in terms of overall patterns of kinship, sociobiological expectations are approximated. Further, the incidence of polygyny as the preferential marriage form in the majority of world cultures (see Murdock, 1967) is also consistent with sociobio-logical expectations. Sahlins' objection would appear to be a case of attempting too literal an interpretation of sociobiology in an attempt to discredit it, ignoring the necessary restraint required in its application to humans.

The charge of the inapplicability of sociobiology to humans due to the uniqueness of humans and of human culture and their ostensible immunity to sixty-five million years of mammalian evolution has a long, illustrious history (Sagan, 1977). Below we will examine the evolutionary continuities of Homo sapiens with other species and consider the uniqueness of human culture and consciousness in relation to other species.

CROSS-SPECIES CONTINUITIES

The extension of sociobiological principles to Homo sapiens requires adherence to specific guidelines and canons of appli-cation. In cross-species comparisons of behavior, the taxonomic relationship of the species in question are of primary importance. Behavioral comparisons are best made between species that have a close phylogenetic relationship. Many of the objections to in-terspecific comparisons of human and other primate behavior are predicated on the assumption that a sharp discontinuity exists between the two (cf. Allen, 1976). As Wilson (1975) notes, we must examine behavioral traits that are constant at the taxonomic level of family. As Homo sapiens are currently classified in a separate family from the great apes, this is taken as *prima facie* evidence against the possibility of interspecific comparisons. However, contemporary taxonomists (e.g., Anderson and Jones, 1967; Vaughan, 1972) indicate that if current standards of tax-onomic classification were applied to man, Homo sapiens would be included with the great apes and gibbons in a single family. The present classification of man in a separate family appears to reflect more the conceit of earlier taxonomists than it does com-pelling and substantive taxonomic differences at the level of clas-sification.

While taxonomic or morphological similarity between man and ape may be conceded, many would argue that a true radical dis-continuity exists in terms of consciousness and mental experience of the two species. While empirical "proof" of the conscious states of nonhumans is difficult to establish, the simple assumption that animals do not have consciousness must be challenged.

Griffin (1976) suggests that it would be more sensible, given physiological similarities between man and apes, to assume that higher primates have at least qualitatively similar mental experiences. Awareness and consciousness confer adaptive advantages to animals by allowing them to react to appropriate physical and biological symbols and events (Thorpe, 1974; Griffin, 1976; see also Popper, 1972). Further, animal communication systems share basic properties with human language, major differences being those of quantity and elaborateness, rather than of the conscious intent to communicate (Griffin 1976; Hall and Sharp, 1978).

Further justification for Griffin's position may be found in the efforts to teach chimpanzees to use American Sign Language (ASL). The Gardners (1969) report a demonstrated capability of chimpanzees to learn ASL and to invent new constructions and words. Chimpanzees were well able to create new phrases and words, to ask questions and to deny assertions put to them.[1] Given the abilities shown by chimpanzees in learning to communicate via ASL and certain computer setups, Sagan (1977) indicates it is difficult to say what the qualitative difference is between the use of language by chimpanzees and that of young children to whom we freely admit consciousness and intelligence. The evidence seems to indicate certain patterns of continuity between humans and apes in at least these areas.

Given the possibility of certain morphological and physiological continuities, the question of behavioral continuity must be raised. The issue becomes one of homology versus analogy. Homologues are, in this matter, similarities in behaviors (interspecific) that are the result of common ancestry (Simpson, 1961). Analogues, on the other hand, refer to similar behavioral characteristics acquired independently (convergent evolution) (Wallace, 1973). A goal of sociobiology is to determine homologies in cross-species behavior, rather than simple analogies (although analogies can be informative in a functional perspective). The identification of homologies lends greater credence to the assertion that genotype is involved in the behavior in question (de Beer, 1958).

To establish homologies, it is necessary to begin with taxonomically related species (Wilson, 1975). Even then, of course, similarities in behavior between closely related species may still be only analogous. Difficulties in establishing interspecific behavioral homology magnify in proportion to the increased role of learning in the species' specific behavior (Wallace, 1973). If we are to compare the behavior of the great apes with humans, care is needed in establishing behaviors that may be considered homologous.

Ethnologists and sociobiologists who have sought to analyze human social behavior through interspecific comparison have failed to observe either restraint or methodological rigor in their dramatic analogies (e.g., Lorenz, 1966). Some anthropologists have taken important steps in establishing homologous links between the behaviors of apes and early hominids (Sahlins, 1959; Callan, 1970). While establishing homologies may be of importance, it must remembered that the absence of homology does not necessarily imply that the behavior does not have an inherited component (Van den Berghe, 1975b).

A second factor in interspecific behavioral comparisons involves the types of behaviors being considered and the levels of social aggregation that are in reference. To establish meaningful cross-species comparisons, behavioral traits must be identified that are common at the taxonomic level of family. Wilson (1975) suggests common traits for primates would include aggressive dominance systems with males dominant, prolonged maternal care and intensive socialization of the young. Cross-species behaviors should be selected and compared that are subsumed within these general categories of behavioral traits. Thus, behaviors to be compared most likely will be at lower levels of social aggregation.

DIFFERENTIAL REPRODUCTION AND INCLUSIVE FITNESS

A sociological interest in sociobiology must be based not only in the realm of cross-species comparisons of social behavior, but also in regard to human behaviors that can be illuminated by principles of differential reproduction. Sociobiology holds that organisms will act in such a way as to maximize their inclusive fitness relative to conspecifics in a given locale (Barash, 1977). That individuals act to promote the survival of kin and progeny becomes the basis for explaining a number of areas of the social behavior of animals, particularly altruism (Wilson, 1975) and parental strategies (Trivers, 1972). At least six behavioral foci can be identified for humans that warrant investigation under the rubric of inclusive fitness. These include: sexual competition for mates, incest avoidance, patterns of group living, nepotism, reciprocity and parenting (Alexander, 1975).

To the extent that such behaviors have a genetic component in their ultimate causation, sociobiology would predict that selection would favor individuals who increased their fitness by assisting closer kin more than distant kin, as well as kin in general more than nonkin, irrespective of the chances of reciprocity (Hamilton, 1964; Trivers, 1971; Alexander, 1975; Barash, 1977). In general, such behaviors are a characteristic part of human kinship relations (e.g., Reiss, 1962; Bott, 1957; Adams, 1968; Van den Berghe, 1980) but given the importance of learning and cultural variations, specific divergences are numerous (Sahlins, 1976). The central question is to what extent are culturally evolved and transmitted prescriptions regarding kin genotypic in origin. The study of cultural universals (Murdock, 1967) may offer further insights into human behaviors that may be predisposed toward genotype. The incest taboo, a universal prohibition in some degree in all cultures, reflects a practice consistent with the prinicple of inclusive fitness. Because incest reduces the inclusive fitness of organisms, its avoidance provides a clear adaptive advantage in an evolutionary sense (Barash, 1977, 1979; Van den Berghe, 1978, 1980).

Reproductive strategies, in terms of differential parental investments (Trivers, 1972), can be compared to general cultural practices to evaluate a possible genotypic role in the behavior. Polygyny as the preferential marriage system (Daly and Wilson, 1978) is consistent, as noted above, with predictions regarding the mating behavior of individuals that are certain of their genetic relation to offsprings (that is, females) and those that are not. Again, the referent is the ultimate or evolutionary source of a behavioral predisposition, not the proximate or culturally learned behavior itself.

SOCIOBIOLOGY, SOCIOLOGY AND THE MICROORDER

Thus far several points have been argued in regard to the use of sociobiology in sociology. Behaviors that are universal or near universal across cultures are more likely to have a genotypic component than more idiosyncratic cultural traits or practices. To compare behaviors across species, it is most fruitful to consider behaviors that are similar between species and to consider behaviors between taxonomically related species. If the species are not taxonomically close, then the species should occupy similar positions in the ecosystem (for example, social apex predators should be compared with other social apex predators). Behaviors must be compared across similar levels of social aggregation or group size.

The past misuses of Darwinian evolutionary theories have been the result of the failure to consider the preceding points. For example, complex modes of the social organization of humans are compared with the territorial behavior of a species that lives in small groups (e.g., Ardrey, 1966). Such behaviors are scarcely analogous. Aggression and territoriality are linked improperly and then ascribed to humans (e.g, Lorenz, 1966) instead of recognizing that the latter reduces the need for the former. Evolutionary principles are applied to the grand movement of societies from one level to a more complex, and implicitly "better," level (e.g., Parsons, 1966), ignoring biogenetic and social levels at which Darwinian theory actually applies and so on.

The behaviors that should be of concern to a human sociobiology are the behaviors that among higher mammals characterize small social aggregates, for example, prides, packs, troops and families. The attempts of the ethological popularizers and the sociobiological vulgarizers (and here Wilson [1978] shares guilt) to explain the social behavior of mass societies of humans are ill founded, however intuitively appealing they might be. The concern of sociobiology must instead be directed toward the human microorder and the processes that create and maintain these basic social solidarities.

Collins (1975) has properly argued that Darwinian theory as applied to humans constitutes a micromodel and must be used as such. In this light, the issues human sociobiology might address include:

1. What is the nature of human social bonding?
2. What are its foundations in a biogenetic and evolutionary sense?
3. In what ways is it analogous to the bonding and ritualized behavior of other mammals?
4. In what ways is it homologous to the bonding and ritualized social behavior of other mammals?
5. What are the interactive processes by which these primal bonds are established and maintained?
6. In what ways is human social behavior on the microlevel consistent with principles of differential reproduction and the maximization of inclusive fitness?

These questions are the domain of a human sociobiology and, as such, neither undermine sociological explanations nor necessarily replace them but rather will add to their depth and explanatory power. The adversary relationship between the two sciences is an artifact of misunderstanding on the part of sociologists and overstatement and misstatement on the part of sociobiologists.

To examine human bonding, sociobiologists should look to the microprocesses of bondings as seen in family and kin groups, as well as to the ritualized and gestural behavior of humans (Collins, 1975). Durkheim (1948) suggested the importance of ritual in creating and maintaining a basic social solidarity, a collective conscience. These social ties involve the effects of stereotyped postures, sounds and gestures. The basic infrastructure of human solidarity is rooted in a biogenetic capacity and predisposition for bonding. Human society as such is subhuman (Collins, 1975), or perhaps more properly, precultural, in its foundation. Culture has facilitated the elaboration of human social organization, but it is grounded in this suggested infrastructure of primal bonding rooted in our evolutionary history. Culture is not a prerequisite of human bonding or human social organization. Durkheim's (1953) suggestion that social interaction forms a substratum out of which collective representations and social solidarity emerge is consistent with this notion.

Humans are by no means unique in their use of ritualized behavior, greeting ceremonies or ceremonies that facilitate solidarity through emotional contagion. Certainly the grooming rituals, deference displays and agonistic displays of higher primates (Schaller, 1963) are at least analogous to, if not homologous with, those of humans in comparable social groups, for example, family or band. The greeting rituals and howling sessions of wolves (Hall and Sharp, 1978) promote solidarity and bonding among wolves in a manner analogous to those of human ceremonies relying on stereotyped behaviors and affective contagion (cf. Durkheim, 1948). (As both wolves and humans occupy positions as apex predators in their ecosystems, to look at analogies in behavior can offer insights into the nature of certain human social practices [e.g., Sharp, 1978; King, 1980].)

It has been characteristic of social scientists to label the stereotyped rituals of humans, from deference displays to greetings to ceremonies, as cultural. Yet the same rituals among other social animals are judged to be predominantly innate. There is, in fact, ample evidence of protocultural rituals, traditions and innovations among higher social species (Itani, 1958; Kawai, 1965; Harding and Strum, 1976; Hall and Sharp, 1978). The possibility is equally present that basic forms of human bonding, as well as other human behaviors such as dominance and deference gestures, agonistic and emotional responses, may be, as Collins (1975:101) indicates, "more innate than we like to believe."

While much of this section has been of necessity speculative, we can point to some work that has been done on these primal aspects of human bonding as they occur within the family. Lorenz's use of the "infant schema" in examining how pedomorphic shapes act as behavioral releasers, eliciting protective behaviors among humans, is one such example (Tinbergen, 1951). Rossi (1978) has reviewed current endocrinological research to establish the biological underpinnings of mother-child bonding and its social implications. Freedman (1979) has conducted research on human infants that has interesting implications for the sociobiological interpretation of human behavior. Similarly, a new journal, *Ethology and Sociobiology*, is presenting much recent human sociobiological research and is evidence of the rapid growth of research in the area.

IMPLICATIONS AND CONCLUSIONS

While this essay has attempted to present evidence which justifies a place for the sociobiological study of humans, caution and
methodological rigor must be observed in its application. The
negative impact of the work of the ethological popularizers has
been adequately documented. The failure to consider species
characteristics, levels of social aggregation and behavioral equiv-
alence have flawed these works. We have provided preliminary
suggestions stipulating some of the necessary conditions for engaging in cross-species behavioral comparisons.

The problems of developing a legitimate sociobiological perspective within sociology are formidable, both in terms of theoretical integration and the generation of data. The gap between
sociobiology and "conventional" sociology is large and is only
deepened by overzealous claims of the usurpation of sociology
by biology (e.g., Wilson, 1975; Ellis, 1977). It has been suggested
here that the domain of a human sociobiology must be restricted
to the microorder of human behavior (Collins, 1975), one with a
strong pan-cultural emphasis. Ritualized and gestural behaviors
would form one focus of this research. To begin a sociobiological
theory at the microlevel is also consistent with Alexander's (1975)
proposal for a general theory of behavior (see also Callan, 1970).

The reluctance of sociologists to pursue a sociobiological perspective will in no way inhibit biologists from promulgating their
own theories of human behavior (cf. Wickler, 1973; Alexander,
1975; Wilson, 1975; Wilson, 1978). Even these most recent theories (e.g., Wilson, 1978; Barash, 1979) would appear premature
in their scope and claims of genetypic involvement in behaviors.
Wilson's most recent human sociobiology, while admittedly very
speculative, marks his attempt to further support the issues raised
in his Chapter 27. While he undoubtedly mounts impressive evidence, his data are nevertheless just suggestive, not necessarily
irrefutable. The book is flawed to a certain extent, in our view,
by a rather naive attack on Marxism, an attack not likely to put
Wilson in good stead with a number of sociologists. The attack
is unfortunate because it further politicizes sociobiology, in addition to demonstrating that Wilson's knowledge of Marxism is
limited indeed. Equally unfortunate is the fact that Wilson has

justified some of the charges of his critics, charges that prior to this recent work were ostensibly false. Barash's recent work covers essentially the same ground as Wilson's although Barash does not grind the same political axe as Wilson. Both books are written for popular audiences, although it would appear the sociobiology would have been served better at this point by a more serious and technical scientific work rather than books somewhat in the vein of the "ethologizers" of the 1960's.

More serious involvement of sociologists in these theoretical attempts might result in a greater restraint on the part of biologists. Unfortunately, the bald assertion that sociobiology is not applicable to humans (e.g., Quadagno, 1979) is not likely to serve any scientific purpose. We have asserted that there is a sufficient basis in terms of Homo sapiens' physiological and morphological continuities with other primates to examine homologous and analogous behaviors cross-specifically. Similarly, basic evolutionary principles of differential reproduction and the maximization of inclusive fitness warrant investigations of their explanatory power for general modes of human cultural and social organization.

Toward these ends it must be accepted that initial steps will, of necessity, be speculative and involve substantial, if justifiable, inferential leaps. However, as Kaplan (1964) indicates, we must be able to entertain an hypothesis before we can test it, perhaps even before we know if it is possible to test it. In this sense, rejection of human sociobiology must be considered premature and without good foundation.

Sociobiology represents a comprehensive theoretical body grounded in Darwinian evolutionary principles, but it is only beginning to be tested even in a rudimentary fashion in regard to humans. Methods do not as yet exist that will allow complete testing of all its aspects. Sociobiology's applicability must be evaluated at the level of the human microorder, not at macroscopic levels in which, as Wilson (1977) notes, the greatest discrepancies between genetic and cultural fitness will be found. Nor is a human sociobiology likely to develop from looking at specific instances of human behavior and trying to explain each by reference to the selective advantage it confers (Wilson, 1978). The intent of a human sociobiology should be, as Gould (1976:28) writes, to "seek a biological basis in generating rules of human behavior, not in specific actions." This essay has suggested that the generic forms of human interaction and social behavior as found in the microorder are the proper focus of a human sociobiology.

NOTE

1. Chimpanzee language research has recently been embroiled in controversy. Critics have questioned the validity of much of the research. Proponents have countered the charges with complex experimental designs intended to preclude cue giving by handlers.

REFERENCES

Adams, B. *Kinship in an Urban Setting*. Markham, Chicago, 1968.

Alexander, R. The search for a general theory of behavior. *Behav. Sci.* 20:77-98, 1975.

Alland, A., Jr. *Evolution and Human Behavior*. Natural History Press, New York, 1967.

Allen, L., and the Sociobiology Study Group of Science for the People. Sociobiology—Another biological determinism. *Bioscience 26*:182-86, 1976.

Anderson, S., and Jones, J.K., Jr. (Eds.). *Recent Mammals of the World*. Ronald Press Co., New York, 1967.

Ardrey, R. *The Territorial Imperative*. Athenaeum, New York, 1966.

Barash, D.P. *Sociobiology and Behavior*. Elsevier, North Holland, New York, 1977.

Barash, D. *The Whisperings Within*. Harper and Row, New York, 1979.

Bolin, R., and Bolin, S.B. Sociobiology and paradigms in evolutionary theory. *Am. Soc. Rev. 54*:154-59, 1980.

Bott, E. *Family and Social Network*. Tavistock, London, 1957.

Callan, H. *Ethology and Society*. Oxford University Press, London, 1970.

Collins, R. *Conflict Sociology*. Academic Press, New York, 1975.

Daly, M., and Wilson, M. *Sex, Evolution and Behavior*. Duxbury, North Scituate, MA, 1978.

de Beer, G.R. *Embryos and Ancestors*, 3rd Ed. Oxford University Press, London, 1958.

Durkheim, E. *The Elementary Forms of Religious Life*. Free Press, New York, 1948.

Durkheim, E. *Sociology and Philosophy*. Free Press, New York, 1953.

Eckberg, D. Sociobiology and the death of sociology: An analytical reply to Ellis. *Am. Sociol. 12*:191-95, 1977.

Ellis, L. The decline and fall of sociology. *Am. Sociol.* 12:77-80, 1977.

Fischer, C. The myth of territoriality in Van den Berghe's Bringing the Beasts Back In. *Am. Soc. Rev.* 40:674-76, 1975.

Freedman, D.G. *Human Sociobiology.* Free Press, New York, 1979.

Gardner, R.A., and Gardner, B.T. Teaching sign language to a chimpanzee. *Science* 165:664-76, 1969.

Gould, S.J. Darwin's untimely burial. *Nat. Hist.* 85:24-30, 1976.

Gould, S.J. *Ever Since Darwin.* Norton, New York, 1977a.

Gould, S.J. *Ontogeny and Phylogeny.* Belknap Press of the Harvard University Press, Cambridge, 1977b.

Griffin, D. *The Question of Animal Awareness.* Rockefeller University Press, New York, 1976.

Hall, R., and Sharp, H. (Eds.). *Wolf and Man.* Academic Press, New York, 1978.

Hamilton, W.D. The genetical evolution of social behavior: Parts I and II. *J. Theor. Biol.* 7:1-51, 1964.

Hamilton, W.D. The genetical theory of social behavior, I and II. *J. Theor. Biol.* 7:1-52, 1976.

Harding, R.S.O., and Strum, S.C. The predatory baboons of Kekopey. *Nat. Hist.* 85:46-53, 1976.

Herrick, C.J. *The Evolution of Human Nature.* University of Texas Press, Austin, 1956.

Hinde, R.A., and Tinbergen, N. The comparative study of species-specific behavior. In: *Behavior and Evolution.* A. Roe and G.G. Simpson (Eds.), Yale University Press, New Haven, CT, pp. 251-68, 1958.

Itani, J. On the acquisition and propagation of a new habit in the natural group of Japanese monkeys at Takasaki-Yama. *Primates* 6:84-98, 1958 (in Japanese with English summary).

Kaplan, A. *The Conduct of Inquiry.* Chandler, Scranton, PA, 1964.

Kawai, M. Newly acquired pre-cultural behavior of the natural troop of Japanese monkeys on Koshima Islet. *Primates* 6:1-30, 1965.

King, G. Alternative uses of primates and carnivores in the reconstruction of early hominid behavior. *Ethol. Sociobiol.* 1:151-62, 1980.

Lorenz, K. The comparative method in studying innate behaviour patterns. *Symp. Soc. Exper. Biol.* 4:221-67, 1950.

Lorenz, K. *On Aggression.* Methuen, London, 1966.

Mayr, E. *Animal Species and Evolution.* Harvard University Press, Cambridge, 1963.

Mayr, E. *Evolution and the Diversity of Life.* Harvard University Press, Cambridge, MA, 1976.

Mazur, A. Cross species comparisons of aggression. *Am. Soc. Rev.* 40:677-78, 1975.

Moberg, D. A comment on Van den Berghe's biosocial model of aggression. *Am. Soc. Rev.* 40:676-77, 1975.

Morris, D. *The Naked Ape.* McGraw-Hill, New York, 1967.

Murdock, G.P. World ethnographic sample. *Am. Anthropol.* 59:664-87, 1967.

Parsons, T. *Societies: Evolutionary and Comparative Perspectives.* Prentice-Hall, Englewood Cliffs, NJ, 1966.

Parsons, T.; Bales, R.; and Shills, E. *Working Papers and the Theory of Action.* Free Press, New York, 1953.

Popper, K. *Objective Knowledge: An Evolutionary Approach.* Clarendon Press, Oxford, England, 1972.

Quadagno, J. Paradigms in evolutionary theory: The sociobiological model of natural selection. *Am. Soc. Rev.* 44:100-09, 1979.

Reiss, P. The extended kinship system: Correlates of and attitudes on frequency of interaction. *Marriage Fam. Liv.* 24:333-39, 1962.

Rossi, A. A biosocial perspective on parenting. In: *The Family.* A. Rossi, J. Kagan and T. Hareven (Eds.), Norton, New York, pp. 1-31, 1978.

Sagan, C. *Dragons of Eden.* Random House, New York, 1977.

Sahlins, M.D. The social life of monkeys, apes, and primitive man. In: *The Evolution of Man's Capacity for Culture.* J.N. Spuhler (Ed.), Wayne State University, Detroit, MI, pp. 54-73, 1959.

Sahlins, M.D. *The Use and Abuse of Biology.* University of Michigan Press, Ann Arbor, 1976.

Schaller, G. *The Mountain Gorilla.* University of Chicago Press, Chicago, 1963.

Science Briefing. 196:4332, 1978.

Scott, J.P. (Ed.). Methodology and techniques for the study of animal societies. *Ann. NY Acad. Sci.* 51:1001-1122, 1950.

Sharp, H. Comparative ethnology of the wolf and the chipewyan. In: *Wolf and Man.* R. Hall and H. Sharp (Eds.), Academic Press, New York, pp. 59-79, 1978.

Simpson, G.G. *Principles of Animal Taxonomy.* Columbia University Press, New York, 1961.

Stent, G. *Paradoxes of Progress.* Freeman, San Francisco, 1978.

Suttles, G. *The Social Construction of Communities.* University of Chicago Press, Chicago, 1972.

Suttles, G. Exchange: Further on sociobiology. *Am. Sociol.* 12:190-99, 1977.

Thorpe, W.H. *Animal Nature and Human Nature.* Anchor-Doubleday, Garden City, NY, 1974.

Tiger, L., and Fox, R. *The Imperial Animal.* Dell, New York, 1971.

Tinbergen, N. *The Study of Instinct*. Oxford University Press, Oxford, England, 1951.

Trivers, R.L. The evolution of reciprocal altruism. *Q. Rev. Biol.* 23:801-25, 1971.

Trivers, R.L. Parental investment and sexual selection. In: *Sexual Selection and the Descent of Man*. B. Campbell (Ed.), Aldine, Chicago, pp. 136-79, 1972.

Van den Berghe, P. Bringing the beasts back in: Toward a biosocial theory of aggression. *Am. Soc. Rev.* 39:778-88, 1974.

Van den Berghe, P. *Man in Society*. Elsevier, New York, 1975a.

Van den Berghe, P. Reply to Fischer, Moberg and Mazur. *Am. Soc. Rev.* 40:678-82, 1975b.

Van den Berghe, P. *Man in Society*, 2d ed., Elsevier, New York, 1978.

Van den Berghe, P. Incest and exogamy. *Ethol. Sociobiol.* 1:151-62, 1980.

Vaughan, T.A. *Mammalogy*. W.B. Saunders Co., Philadelphia, 1972.

Wallace, R.A. *Ecology and the Evolution of Animal Behavior*. Goodyear, Pacific Palisades, CA, 1973.

Wickler, W. *The Sexual Code*. Anchor, Garden City, NY, 1973.

Williams, G.C. *Adaptation and Natural Selection*. Princeton University Press, Princeton, NJ, 1966.

Wilson, E.O. Prospects for a unified sociobiology. *Am. Sci.* 59:400-17, 1971.

Wilson, E.O. *Sociobiology: The New Synthesis*. The Belknap Press of Harvard University Press, Cambridge, MA, 1975.

Wilson, E.O. Academic vigilantism and the political significance of sociobiology. *Bioscience* 26:183-90, 1976.

Wilson, E.O. *On Human Nature*. Harvard University Press, Cambridge, MA, 1978.

2

Hierarchical Differentiation in Newly Formed Groups of Rhesus and Humans

Patricia R. Barchas and M. Hamit Fisek

Hierarchies are a regularly occurring form of social organization of relationship in which group members are differentiated one from the other in a more or less linear fashion. The ease with which this particular form of social organization develops in most species of primates invites comparative study. Social hierarchies are characterized by phases of emergence, maintenance, and decay or change. This chapter reports a study on the emergent phase of small group formation in triads of two species of primate known to be likely to develop hierarchical relationships under laboratory conditions. Similar observational and analytic methods are used to focus on rate of differentiation of position and stability of occupancy of positions in groups of male college freshmen and in rhesus macaques.

A prevalent form of social organization in human and in other primate groups, social hierarchies apparently serve two functions fundamental to group formation and maintenance. First, they provide a patterned differentiation of group members one from the other such that at least rough coordination of action amongst group members is assured. Indeed, knowledge of how members are located with respect to their group's hierarchical structure tells even an outside observer a lot about how individuals are likely to behave with regard to each other and to the situation at hand. Second, distribution of the group's resources—such as attention, rewards, rights and obligations—often correspond to the hierarchical structure.

The literature on human groups describes two sets of initial conditions from which the relationship between position in the social status order and social behavior may emerge in task-oriented groups. First, culturally recognized forms of social status or diffuse status characteristics (such as race, sex, and occupation) impinge on the behavior and cognitions of task-oriented group members, whether or not the parameters of status are directly related to the parameters of the task (Hurwitz et al., 1965; Katz et al., 1958; Katz et al., 1964; Strodtbeck and Mann, 1956; Strodtbeck et al., 1958; Torrance, 1954). These studies differ in particulars, but they all report observations on the effect of externally defined social inequalities on social interaction and on problem solving. Second, social status has been observed to emerge in task-oriented groups whose members are initially undifferentiated in terms of societal statuses such as age, sex and education (Bales, 1953; Bales et al., 1951; Harvey, 1953; Sherif et al., 1955). Although these researches differ in their particular settings, they all report observations of the formation of inequalities which take place in initially homogeneous groups. (For an unusually lucid set of sociological analyses and explanations of these phenomena, see Berger [1958], Berger et al. [1966], Berger et al. [1977] and Berger et al. [1980].)

Most observations of nonhuman primates have been made on single groups of mixed age and sex. These variables are known to be associated with position in the hierarchy, presumably operating in much the same way—or at least having similar effects— as diffuse status characteristics do in human groups. Observations are usually made on groups in which individuals have interacted over a period of time. There is consensus amongst primatologists that status relationships are importantly correlated with some aspects of social behavior (see Bernstein, 1980;

Erwin, 1979; Rowell, 1974; Wade, 1978). It is often assumed that these relationships are the product of long-term socialization in groups with stable membership and are based either on the familiarity of individuals one with the other or on differentiating characteristics such as age, sex and condition. Familiarity and status characteristics undoubtedly complement and reinforce systems of hierarchical relationships once they exist, but they do not easily account for hierarchical relationships which emerge amongst individuals who are strangers and not initially differentiated.

The remainder of this chapter reports an exploratory investigation of the emergence of status orders over time in both human and nonhuman primate triads on which observations were carried out in comparable fashion. Data are presented from which to assess the assertion that in newly established groups of both human and nonhuman primates orders are established very early in the temporal sequence of events even though group members are strangers and initial differentiating cues are minimal. Under the experimental conditions used, stability of positional occupancy was expected throughout the period of group interaction subsequent to emergence of behavioral differentiation.

PROCEDURES

The data on humans were collected from seventy-six experimental three-person discussion groups (Fisek, 1968). The group members were freshmen students from Stanford University, recruited in classes and paid for their participation in the study. Each group of three was composed such that none of the participants knew each other beforehand, and there was no visible characteristic (such as race) differentiating them. Seventeen of the original seventy-six groups were eliminated from the sample for failing to meet these conditions, leaving fifty-nine groups for which data were analyzed. Each group was given the same discussion problem to work on for forty-five minutes: the construction of a problem suitable for problem-solving groups such as their own. The topic was chosen as the best way to minimize task demands for organization and yet make sure that interaction did take place, thereby approximating free interaction in the laboratory.

The experimental sessions were held in a soundproof laboratory room equipped with sound-recording equipment and one-way mirrors. The entire sessions were tape recorded, as were the data records of the observers. The data recorded were the sequence of acts initiated by each member of the group. Recording was done by two observers independently of each other, and a reasonably good interobserver reliability was obtained (.87).

The choice of "acts initiated" as the basic unit of data was based on a line of studies originating with Bales and his associates (1951). Early on they observed that "marked inequalities develop over time in the rate at which members are observed to initiate interaction (and) those who initiate action most frequently tend to be ranked highest on the criteria of 'best ideas' and 'guidance' and tend to receive actions from others at the highest rate" (p. 144). Since this initial finding, the phenomenon has been further documented in a variety of different contexts and its stability established with little question (Bales, 1953; Bales and Slater, 1955; Borgatta and Bales, 1953; Fisek and Ofshe, 1970; Heinicke and Bales, 1953; Berger et al., 1980; Stephan and Mishler, 1952; Berger et al., 1966).

Subsequent studies have documented a high degree of correlation between various behavioral dimensions (such as frequency of initiation of acts, frequency of reception of acts, action opportunities, length of speech, and perceptions of "leadership," "guidance," and "liking"), which, taken together, constitute the general notion of status used (Bales, 1953). Of these different dimensions, frequency of initiation has the advantage of being the most easily observed and hence the most replicable, involving the least subjective data collection techniques.

The data on the primates were collected from a total of thirteen experimental groups of three animals each, of which nine were adult female and four were adult male rhesus macaques (Barchas, 1971). The animals had been captured from various ongoing social groups in India and had arrived in this country no earlier than six weeks nor later than two weeks prior to observation. Each experimental group was composed so that it was unlikely that any of the three animals knew each other beforehand. In

each group animals were matched so that no visible characteristics such as age, size, physical condition, or sexual receptivity
differentiated them, so far as could be determined by the experienced veterinarian who handled, evaluated and matched them.
They were housed apart from each other until twenty minutes
prior to the observations; at that time the cages were brought
into the observation room. Observation sessions were begun by
releasing the three animals simultaneously by use of a pulley
system which opened the guillotine-type doors.

Observations were recorded through a one-way mirror for sixty
minutes after the opening of the cages. Acts which typically have
been described as reflecting either dominance or submission
(Chance, 1956) were sequentially recorded according to actor and
recipient. For this analysis, in order to emphasize comparability
of the data, only the initiator of acts is considered. However,
dominant acts are considered separately from submissive-deferent acts.

DATA

In order to determine whether a status order is established in
these groups as demonstrated by the rates of initiation of dominant and submissive acts in the case of the rhesus and the rate
of the initiation of acts in the case of the humans, the overall rates
of emitting dominant acts and emitting submissive acts for each
rank in the rhesus groups were calculated along with the overall
rate of initiating all acts for each position in the human groups.

Table 2.1 displays the mean values of the indices for each rank,
determined by the value of each index averaged over all the groups
in each study (rhesus $N = 13$, humans $N = 59$). Column 2 gives
the values of rate of initiation of dominant acts. The value of the
index is 61.2 percent for the first rank, 31.0 percent for the second
rank, and 18.8 percent for the third rank. Clearly, considerable
differentiation exists in the values of the index for each rank.
Column 3 gives the rate of initiation of submissive acts for each
rank. Once again, considerable differentiation exists in the values
of this index for each rank. The value of the index is 74.6 percent
for the first rank, 20.8 percent for the second rank, and 4.6 percent
for the third rank. Column 4 displays exactly the analogous in-

Table 2.1
Status Indices for Each Structural Rank

Rank	Rate of Initiating Dominant Acts[*] (Rhesus N=13)	Rate of Initiating Submissive Acts[+] (Rhesus N=13)	Rate of Initiating Acts[‡] (Humans N=59)
1	.612	.746	.410
2	.310	.208	.344
3	.188	.046	.246

[*]Rank 1 indicates animal with highest rate of initiating dominant acts.

[+]Rank 1 indicates animal with highest rate of initiating submissive acts.

[‡]Rank 1 indicates human with highest rate of initiating acts.

formation for the case of the Homo sapiens: the overall rates of initiation of acts for each rank in the system are given. This is the indicator used to parallel the rates of initiating dominant and submissive acts in the case of the rhesus groups. A straightforward examination of the values of the interaction rates for the ranks reveals that they display the same pattern observed in the case of the rhesus. It is clear, however, that the differentiation in the values of the indices is considerably less for the human groups than for the rhesus.

It should be emphasized that the rank of each animal for both dimensions is determined by the total number of his output of dominant and deferent acts, respectively, and that the rank of each human is determined by the total number of initiated acts. Simply by the way these ranks are determined, the subject which holds rank 1 on the dimension would be expected to have a higher rate than subjects which hold second and third ranks, and the second-ranked subject to have a higher rate than the third-ranked subject. However, the basic point here is not that there is a difference between the ranks on each dimension, but that the difference is larger than what would be expected by chance if there were no real differentiation among the subjects. It is therefore necessary to demonstrate that the differences in the rates observed for each rank are different from what would be expected by chance, for both the rhesus and human groups. To do this, a chi-square test was performed for each index. The results of these tests are reported in Table 2.2.

Column 2 gives the results of the test as performed on the distribution of the number of dominant acts for each rank for the rhesus groups. The chi-square calculated separately for each group is significant for eleven of the thirteen groups in the sample. For the two groups where the value of the chi-square is not significant at the .05 level, the actual chi-square values are 5.4 and 2.0. Since the chi-square is additive, the chi-squares for each group are added to obtain a single value for the entire sample. Doing so yields the value of 365.03. With 26 degrees of freedom (each individual group chi-square has 2 degrees of freedom), this chi-square is much greater than what would be needed for sample significance at the .001 level, which is 54.05. Performing a chi-square test in exactly the same way as was done in the case of the dominance index, we obtain the results that the difference in the rates of initiation of submissive acts is significant at the .05 level for twelve groups out of the sample of thirteen. The group where the value of the chi-square does not reach significance at the .05 level has a value of 4.6. Summing the chi-squares for each group, the total chi-square value of 619.11 is obtained, considerably greater than the value needed to achieve significance at the .001 level with 26 degrees of freedom. The results are reported in column 3 of Table 2.2. On the basis of this test, column 4 shows that differentiation in forty-seven of the fifty-nine human groups is significant at the .05 level. In the remaining twelve groups of the sample the differentiation did not achieve significance at the .05 level. Summing the values of the chi-squares across groups, a total chi-square value of 1,429.5 with 18 degrees of freedom is

Table 2.2
Chi-Square Test of the No Differentiation between Ranks
Hypothesis for the Status Indices for Rhesus and for Humans

	Rate of Initiating Dominant Acts (Rhesus $\underline{N}$=13)	Rate of Initiating Submissive Acts (Rhesus $\underline{N}$=13)	Rate of Initiating Acts (Humans $\underline{N}$=59)
Number of groups significant at 0.05 level	11 (85%)	12 (92%)	47 (80%)
Number of groups not significant at 0.05 level	2	1	12
Sum of chi-squares for entire sample	365.03	619.11	1,429.5
Degrees of freedom	26	26	118
Associated significance level	<.001	<.001	<.001

obtained. This value is greater than that required for significance at the .001 level, supporting the contention that the observed differentiation in human groups is not by chance.

In these samples of rhesus and human groups, the observed differentiation seems to be much more pronounced for the rhesus than for the humans. However, the basic pattern of differentiation of initiated acts is similar in both cases, supporting the notion that a differentiated order exists amongst the actors making up the group, whether they be rhesus or human. Given that differentiation, questions of stability over time and speed of emergence can be addressed. Two ways were used to determine whether the order is stable over the time of observation. First, the rates of initiating dominant and submissive acts in the case of the rhesus and the overall rate of initiation of acts in the case of the humans are graphed over time. Second, a rank-order correlation of the ranks of the actors in sequential periods during the group session is calculated. For the rhesus groups the rates of initiating dominant acts and the rates of initiating submissive acts are calculated for each rank for periods of fifteen minutes each. This gives three points covering the group sessions. The values of the rates of initiating dominant acts are given in Figure 2.1.

Each graph in the figure represents one positional rank. The important fact to note about the figure is that the curves display trends, providing us with information about the emergence of a status structure in the groups. Quite clearly, the rate of initiating dominant acts increases for the top-ranking animal. During the first fifteen-minute interval, it is 48 percent; during the last fifteen-minute interval, this value increases to 69 percent. For the second-ranking animal, the value of this index at first is 42 percent and decreases to 28 percent during the last fifteen-minute interval. The value of this index for the third-ranking animal is rather flat over time, although it does show a slight decrease from 10 percent during the first time interval to 3 percent in the last time interval. On the basis of these curves, it seems that the development of a differentiated structure in the group is reflected by the rate of the initiation of dominant acts.

Figure 2.2 presents the curves for the rates of initiation of submissive acts for each rank in a manner analogous to the presentation in Figure 2.1. The picture presented by this index is quite

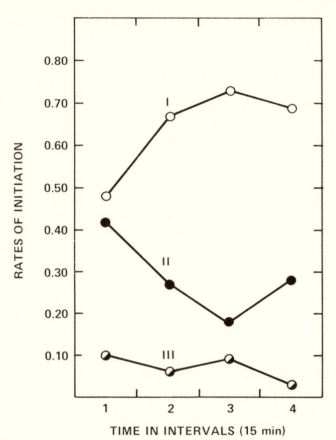

Figure 2.1 Rates of initiating dominant acts for fifteen-minute intervals
based on dominance ranking: Rhesus.

similar to that of the first index. The three curves do not overlap
at any point and show developmental trends over time. The submission rate for the most submissive actor increases over time,
but it decreases for the other two actors.

Analogously, for the human groups the rates of interaction
associated with each rank are calculated for sequential periods
of nine minutes each, giving five data points covering the group
sessions. The values of this interaction rate are graphed in Figure

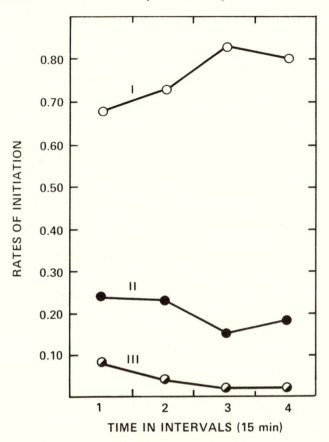

Figure 2.2 Rates of initiating submissive acts for fifteen-minute intervals based on submissive ranking: Rhesus.

2.3. Each curve corresponds to one rank. As was the case for the rhesus, the curves do not overlap at any point. Unlike the rhesus, differentiation does not increase over time but is immediately stable.

Characterization of each status rank by the indices used seems stable over time for both kinds of groups. However, it is readily apparent that the almost flat curves for the Homo sapiens do not show the developmental trends which can be observed in the

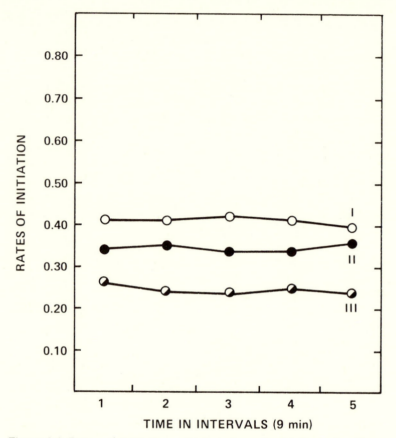

Figure 2.3 Rates of initiating acts for nine-minute intervals: Homo
        sapiens.

curves for the rhesus groups. This question will be re-examined
after further evidence on the stability of these ranks over time is
presented.

   It may be possible that the stability of the status structure represented by the curves in Figures 2.1, 2.2 and 2.3 is brought about
by the process of averaging the values of the indices over groups,
and that the status order of particular groups is not as stable as
the graphs would indicate. To determine whether the order is
indeed stable within particular groups, the following analysis was

carried out. For the rhesus groups, breaking up the sessions into fifteen-minute intervals, the ranking of each actor for both indices was calculated independently for each period. Then within each group a rank concordance coefficient between the ranks was computed in each period both for the ranks of initiating dominant acts and for the ranks of initiating submissive acts. The rank concordance coefficient used is Kendall's W, even though, since we are dealing with a small number of objects ranked a small number of times and the test statistic associated with W is highly discontinuous, the test does not give an accurate picture in cases where the coefficient does not achieve significance. This analysis is repeated in exactly analogous fashion for the human groups by breaking up the sessions into five intervals of nine minutes each.

The results of this analysis are displayed in Table 2.3. Column 2 gives the results for the ranking based on the rate of initiating dominant acts for the rhesus. For five of the thirteen groups, the value of the concordance coefficient is significant at better than the .05 level. For the remaining eight groups, this coefficient does not achieve significance. The average value of W over all groups is .66, and the probability level associated with this value is .15. Column 3 presents the data for ranking based on the rates of initiating submissive acts. In this case, for ten of the thirteen groups the coefficient of concordance is significant at better than the .05 level. With the remaining three groups, significance is not achieved. The average value of W for the thirteen groups is .83, with the associated probability level of .05. Inspection of the data revealed that all groups differentiated by the dominance index were also differentiated by the submissive index, suggesting that either behavior pattern can carry the differentiated process (see Chapters 3 and 4). Column 4 presents the results of the similar analysis carried out for the groups of Homo sapiens. In thirty-four groups of the total sample of fifty-nine, the coefficient of concordance is significant at better than the .05 level. The average value of W across groups is .59, with the associated probability level of .10.

On the basis of the preceding analysis based on Kendall's W, it is reasonable to conclude that the picture of stability of the status order as illustrated by Figures 2.1, 2.2 and 2.3 is partially

Table 2.3
Concordance of Ranks Over Time: Kendall's W

	Dominance Ranks in Four Fifteen-Minute Intervals (Rhesus N=13)	Submission Ranks in Four Fifteen-Minute Intervals (Rhesus N=13)	Initiation Ranks in Five Nine-Minute Intervals (Humans N=59)
Number of groups significant at 0.05 level	5	10	34
Number of groups not significant at 0.05	8	3	25
Average value of W	.66	.83	.59
Probability associated with W	<.125	<.042	<.093

due to artifactual effects obtained through averaging across groups. However, enough genuine stability of the hierarchical order seems to exist to warrant further analysis.

Examining Figures 2.1, 2.2 and 2.3 for developmental trends, we find obvious and clearcut developmental trends for the curves for the two indices for the rhesus which cannot be observed in the curves for the human groups. This is contrary to our expectations, since in the case of both the rhesus and the humans the experimental groups are ad hoc groups of subjects with no previous acquaintance and with no visible discriminating characteristics. Even though in both types of groups subjects have fully developed social repertoires, the status order was expected to emerge after a process of interaction, since there is no apparent basis on which it could emerge on *a priori* grounds. Were this the case, the curves representing the indices for the three status ranks should start out close together and diverge as the status order develops in the group. While the graphs of neither status index for the rhesus start out at the same point, the curves make the hypothesis of developmental emergence tenable. Nevertheless, the initial separation of the starting point for these curves suggests that the process of status-order emergence is very rapid and must occur within the most initial phases of group interaction. In human groups the process does not progress to the same extent as in the rhesus groups, perhaps suggesting there are factors in human task groups which can inhibit, limit, or functionally replace hierarchical differentiation as a principle of social organization.

Speed of emergence may explain the lack of visible developmental trends in the curves for the human groups, a hypothesis which may be approached through further analysis. In order to get a better picture of the developmental situation, it is possible to look at the initial parts of these curves in greater detail, giving some evidence on the question of whether the development of the status structure can be explained as a process over time, presumably arising out of interaction, or whether it is instantaneously established, presumably arising out of prebehavioral mechanisms.

Figures 2.4, 2.5 and 2.6 present the rates of initiating dominant acts and the rates of initiating submissive acts for the rhesus groups and the overall rates of initiating acts for the human groups for three-minute intervals for the first fifteen minutes of the rhesus group sessions and the first nine minutes of the human group session. The curves for the human groups display more trend effects than the original curves. Although the effect is not very large, it is minimally consistent with the development out of interaction hypothesis. The curves for the status indices for the

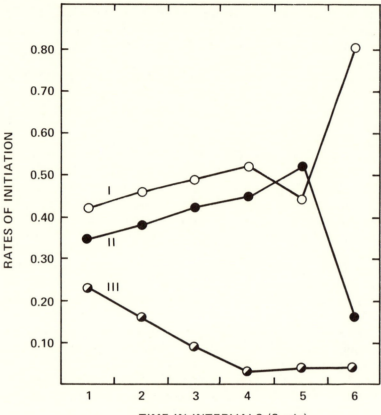

Figure 2.4 Rates of initiating dominant acts for three-minute intervals based on dominance ranking: Rhesus.

rhesus amplify the trends observed earlier. The rhesus curves reflect a process of emergence and development of a hierarchical structure in these groups, which is consistent with the hypothesis that the order is worked out behaviorally through interaction.

To further explore the emergent properties of the differentiation, the chi-squares on the indices were computed for the first fifteen and nine minutes of the sessions for the rhesus and human groups, respectively. The results of this analysis are displayed in

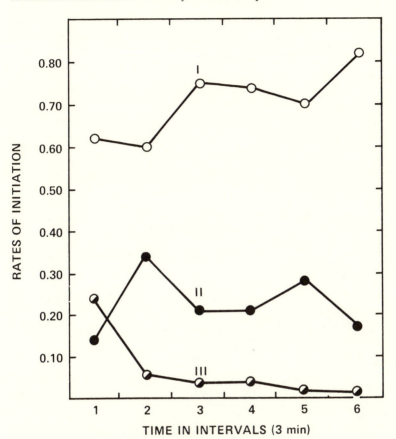

Figure 2.5 Rates of initiating submissive acts for the first fifteen minutes based on submissive ranking: Rhesus.

Table 2.4 and are comparable to the chi-squares computed for differentiation over the entire observation period presented earlier in Table 2.2. Column 1 gives the results of the chi-square test for the rates of initiating dominant acts. In the first fifteen minutes of the group session, we find that nine of the thirteen groups show differentiation significant at the .05 level. Similarly, column 2 gives the results of the chi-square test for the rates of initiating submissive acts. Once again, nine of the thirteen groups display

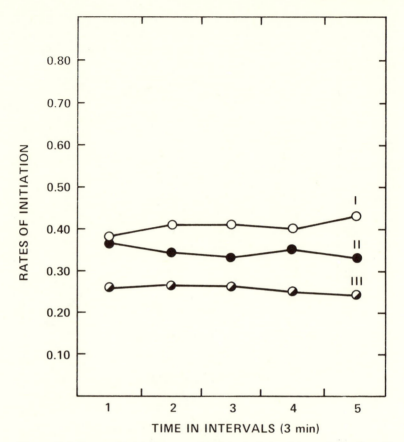

Figure 2.6 Rates of initiating acts for three-minute intervals for first fifteen minutes: Homo sapiens.

statistically significant differentiation. Column 3 presents the data
for the human groups. Forty-seven groups of the total sample of
fifty-nine show differentiation significant at the .05 level.

Almost all of the rhesus groups which were to achieve differentiation by the end of the observation period (85 percent by the
dominance and 92 percent by the submissive-deferent indices)
had done so within the first time period: two more on the dominance and one more group on the submission-deferent indices
differentiated over the remaining time, and all of the early dif-

Table 2.4
Chi-Square Test of the No Differentiation between Ranks
Hypothesis for the Status Indices for Rhesus for the First Fifteen
Minutes and for Humans for the First Nine Minutes

	Rate of Initiating Dominant Acts (Rhesus $N=13$)	Rate of Initiating Submissive Acts (Rhesus $N=13$)	Rate of Initiating Acts (Humans $N=59$)
Number of groups significant at 0.05 level	9	9	47
Number of groups not significant at 0.05 level	4	4	12

ferentiations were maintained. Of the forty-seven human groups which were to achieve differentiation by the end of the observation period (80 percent), all of them had done so by the end of the first time period.

CONCLUSION

The data suggest that in newly formed groups of humans and nonhuman primates, certain aspects of the process of hierarchy formation are similar. Under the conditions of no prior acquaintance of group members and with external status characteristics controlled, differentiation of position tends to occur early in the temporal sequence of events and, once emerged, that differentiation tends to be stable for the duration of observation. Though occurring quickly in both species, differentiation is more rapid in humans. It may be possible to attribute this to the task inherent in human groups, under the assumption that a group goal facilitates group organization. However, it seems more likely that differences between the species in terms of cognitive capacities for processing social information is at issue. For example, the developmental curves apparent in the rhesus groups are consistent with the notion that the emergence of ranked relationships requires interaction (see Chapters 2 and 3), an argument which is strained for the human curves. Also, the degree of differentiation is slight in the human groups compared with the rhesus even though stability is comparable. It may be that under these circumstances, the human capacity for linguistic nuance lessens the requirement for the behavioral differentiation observed in the rhesus groups.

These samples of newly formed triads of rhesus and humans were matched on diffuse status characteristics and had not interacted previously. Yet, hierarchical differentiation tended to occur in both types of groups. The rapidity and apparent ease with which the structures emerged in groups of both species suggest that hierarchical forms of social organization are intrinsic to the social repertoire of primates. It is as if they represent a class of basic strategies for social organization which has been preserved through evolution despite species specific variations on the theme. At the same time, enough variability is apparent even in the rhesus groups to preclude a simple, mechanistic view of the hierarchical differentiation.

REFERENCES

Bales, R.F. The equilibrium problem in small groups. In: *Working Papers in the Theory of Action*. T. Parsons, R.F. Bales and E. Shils (Eds.), Free Press, Glencoe, IL, pp. 111-161, 1953.

Bales, R.F., and Slater, P.E. Role differentiation in small decision making groups. In: *Family, Socialization and Interaction Processes*. T. Parsons and R.F. Bales (Eds.), Free Press, Glencoe, IL, pp. 259-306, 1955.

Bales, R.F.; Strodbeck, F.L.; Mills, T.M.; and Roseborough, M.E. Channels of communication in small groups. *Am. Soc. Rev.* 16:461-68, 1951.

Barchas, P.R. Differentiation and stability of dominance and deference orders in rhesus monkeys. Ph.D. dissertation. Stanford University, 1971.

Berger, J. Relations between Performance, Rewards, and Action Opportunities in Small Groups. Ph.D. dissertation. Harvard University, 1958.

Berger, J.; Cohen, B.P.; Connor, T.; and Zelditch, M., Jr. Status characteristics and expectation states: A process model. In: *Sociological Theories in Progress*, vol. 1. J. Berger, M. Zelditch, Jr., and B. Anderson (Eds.), Houghton Mifflin Company, Boston, pp. 29-46, 1966.

Berger, J.; Fisek, M.H.; Norman, R.A.; and Zelditch, M., Jr. *Status Characteristics and Social Interation: An Expection States Approach*. Elsevier Scientific Publishing Co., New York, 1977.

Berger, J.; Rosenholz, S.J.; and Zelditch, M., Jr. Status organizing processes. *Ann. Rev. Sociology* 6:479-508, 1980.

Bernstein, I.S. Dominance: A theoretical perspective for ethologists. In: *Dominance Relations: An Ethological View of Human Conflict and Social Interaction*. D.R. Omack, F.F. Strayer and D.G. Freedman (Eds.), Garland Press, New York, pp. 71-84, 1980.

Bernstein, I., and Mason, W.A. Group formation by rhesus monkeys. *Br. J. Animal Behav.* 11:28-31, 1963.

Borgatta, E.F., and Bales, R.F. Interaction of individuals in reconstituted groups. *Sociometry* 16:312-20, 1953.

Carpenter, C.R. A field study of the behavior and social relations of howling monkeys, pp. 3-92; Societies of monkeys and apes, pp. 342-64; Characteristics of social behavior in non-human primates, pp. 342-64; and Social behavior of nonhuman primates, pp. 365-84. In: *Naturalistic Behavior of Nonhuman Primates*. C.R. Carpenter (Ed.), Pennsylvania State University, University Park, 1964.

Chance, M.R.A. Social structure of a colony of *Macaca mulatta*. *Br. J. Animal Behav.* 4:1-13, 1956.

DeVore, I. (Ed.). *Primate Behavior: Field Studies of Monkeys and Apes*. Holt, Rinehart and Winston, New York, 1965.

Erwin, J. Aggression in captive macaques: Interaction of social and spatial factors. In: *Captivity and Behavior*. J. Erwin, T.L. Maple and G. Mitchell (Eds.), Van Nostrand Rheinhold Co., New York, pp. 139-71, 1979.

Fisek, M.H. The evolution of status structures and interaction in task oriented discussion groups. Ph.D. dissertation. Stanford University, 1968.

Fisek, M.H., and Ofshe, R. The process of status evolution. *Sociometry* 33:327-46, 1970.

Hall, K.R.L. Social organization of the old-world monkeys and apes. In: *Primates: Studies in Adaptation and Variability*. P. Jay (Ed.), Holt, Rinehart and Winston, New York, pp. 7-31, 1968.

Harvey, O.J. An experimental approach to the study of status relations in informal groups. *Am. Soc. Rev. 18*:357-67, 1953.

Heinicke, C., and Bales, R.F. Developmental trends in the structure of small groups. *Sociometry 16*:7-38, 1953.

Hurwitz, J.I.; Zander, A.F.; and Hymovitch, B. Some effects of power on the relations of group members. In: *Group Dynamics*. D. Cartwright and A. Zander (Eds.), Harper and Row, New York, pp. 448-56, 1965.

Jay, P. Primate field studies and human evolution. In: *Primates:Studies in Adaptation and Variability*. P. Jay (Ed.), Holt, Rinehart and Winston, New York, pp. 487-503, 1968.

Katz, I.; Epps, E.; and Axelson, L. Effect upon Negro digit-symbol performance of anticipated comparison with whites and other Negroes. *J. Abn. Soc. Psychol. 69*:77-83, 1964.

Katz, I.; Goldston, J.; and Benjimin, L. Behavior and productivity in biracial work groups. *Human Relations 11*:123-41, 1958.

Rowell, T.E. The concept of social dominance. *Behav. Biol. 11*:131-54, 1974.

Sherif, M.; White, B. J.; and Harvey, O. J. Status in experimentally produced groups. *Am. J. Soc. 60*:370-79, 1955.

Stephan, F., and Mishler, E.G. The distributions of participation in small groups: An exponential approximation. *Am. Soc. Rev. 17*:598-608, 1952.

Strodtbeck, F.L., and Mann, R.D. Sex role differentiation in jury deliberation. *Sociometry 19*:3-11, 1956.

Strodtbeck, F.L.; James, R.M.; and Hawkins, C. Social status in jury deliberations. In: *Readings in Social Psychology*. E.E. Maccoby,T.M. Newcomb and E.L. Hartley (Eds.), Third Edition, Holt, New York, pp. 379-88, 1958.

Torrance, E.P. Some consequences of power differences on decision making in permanent and temporary three-man groups. *Res. Stud. State Coll. Washington 22*:130-40, 1954.

Wade, T.D. Status and hierarchy in nonhuman primate societies. In: *Perspectives in Ethology*, vol. 3. P.P.G. Bateson and P.H. Klopfa (Eds.), Plenum Press, New York, pp. 109-34, 1978.

3

Social Process and Hierarchy Formation in Small Groups: A Comparative Perspective

Ivan D. Chase

Despite great differences in social behavior in many human and animal groups, their dominance hierarchies are remarkably similar. (See Brown [1975] and Wilson [1975] for general background on dominance hierarchies.) Why should species so diverse as animals are from one another, and as all the animals are from humans, form dominance hierarchies so similar in structure? And, even more basically, how are we to study and explain the formation of dominance structures in small groups of men and animals? The goal here is to make a start toward answering these questions by developing a new approach to the study of hierarchy structures. This approach explains how hierarchies emerge from the interaction among group members rather than being generated by differences among those individuals. It treats

This chapter has been reprinted from *American Sociological Review* 45 (1980):905-24 with the permission of the author and the American Sociological Association.

hierarchy formation as a developmental process in which the outcomes of previous interactions influence the course of successive ones, and it indicates how patterns of interaction fit together to form the kinds of dominance hierarchies commonly observed.

This essay is in five parts: (1) a summary of the data collected on dominance hierarchies and the methods used to gather those data in both the animal behavior and the human social sciences literature; (2) a critical evaluation of the theories that have been proposed to explain hierarchy structures in both disciplines; (3) a presentation of the results of a study of hierarchy formation in an animal group; (4) a new approach to the theory of hierarchy formation; and (5) an evaluation of the new approach as well as a discussion of the implications of the results for continuing research.

HIERARCHY STRUCTURES IN ANIMAL AND HUMAN GROUPS

The Animal Behavior Approach

One of the distinguishing features of the animal behavior or ethological tradition is the emphasis on behavioral observation and the use of ethograms (or catalogs of behavior) developed for each kind of animal or human group studied. In a typical ethological study, a group is observed for a period of time sufficiently long to discover the direction of dominance relationships among all possible pairs in the group. The direction of a dominance relationship in a pair is typically determined by asymmetries in the agonistic (a category including both aggressive and submissive behaviors) behavior of the individuals toward one another. For example, the individual who delivers all or the majority of aggressive acts in a pair is considered dominant, and the individual who receives the acts or initiates most of the submissive gestures is considered subordinate. The pattern of the relationships in a group is frequently represented in a "dominance matrix." A dominance matrix has either a "0" or a "1" in all off-diagonal cells: a "1" in the i, j cell indicates that individual i dominates individual j and a "0" indicates that j dominates i.

All the dominance relationships in a group, taken together, form the hierarchy structure. Theoretically, hierarchy structures can vary from linear, at one extreme, to the other extreme in which each individual in the group dominates an equal number of other individuals. In a linear hierarchy there is an individual *A* who dominates all others, an individual *B* who dominates all but *A*, and so forth, down to the last individual who dominates no one. An example of a dominance matrix for a linear hierarchy with five individuals is given in Table 3.1, and a matrix for a hierarchy as far away from linearity as possible—in which each animal dominates an equal number of animals—is given in Table 3.2.

A surprisingly uniform finding by ethologists is that hierarchies in small groups (less than about ten members) are frequently and perhaps predominantly linear or near linear. This finding is stable across many individual researchers' work and across an extremely broad range of animal species from insects to primates. For example, linear and near-linear hierarchies have been found among certain kinds of wasps and bumble bees (Wilson, 1971); various birds—such as chickens (Guhl, 1975), chaffinches (Marler, 1955), and red crossbills (Tordoff, 1954); domestic mammals— such as cows (Schein and Fohrman, 1955) and ponies (Tyler, 1972); wild mammals—such as coyotes (Bekoff, 1977) and buf-

Table 3.1
Dominance Matrix Showing a Linear Hierarchy

Dominant Animal	Dominated Animal					Number Dominated
	A	B	C	D	E	
A	--	1	1	1	1	4
B	0	--	1	1	1	3
C	0	0	--	1	1	2
D	0	0	0	--	1	1
E	0	0	0	0	--	0

Table 3.2
Dominance Matrix Showing a Hierarchy in Which Each Animal
Dominates an Equal Number of Other Animals

Dominant Animal	Dominated Animal					Number Dominated
	A	B	C	D	E	
A	--	1	1	0	0	2
B	0	--	1	1	0	2
C	0	0	--	1	1	2
D	1	0	0	--	1	2
E	1	1	0	0	--	2

faloes (McHugh, 1975); and primates in the wild and in captivity—including rhesus monkeys (Sade, 1967), baboons (Hausfater, 1975) and vervets (Struhsaker, 1967). In the primates, hierarchies can become more complex through both the formation of coalitions and what is known as dependent rank (Jolly, 1972). In dependent rank, a particular individual (animal) is able to achieve dominance over another animal in the presence of a third animal (frequently its mother or consort) but not able to do so if the third animal is not present. However, even in those groups where coalitions and dependent rank are found, there is often a linear or near-linear hierarchy if relationships are examined between pairs when a coalition partner or third party conferring dependent rank is not present.

Researchers in the ethological tradition who have studied human groups have frequently focused on hierarchical relationships; many of these studies have been on preschool children (McGrew, 1972; Missakian, 1976; Strayer and Strayer, 1976), but adolescent groups have also been examined (Savin-Williams, 1977; 1979; 1980). In addition to using nonverbal, behavioral measures of dominance, as in the animal studies, some studies have also employed verbal indices of dominance—for example, if A gives an order to B and B obeys, then A is rated as dominant to B

(Savin-Williams, 1977; 1979; 1980). As in the animal studies, findings indicate that human hierarchies are frequently linear or near linear (Missakian, 1976; Savin-Williams, 1977; 1979; 1980). In those studies where data have been collected for some but not all possible pair-wise interactions, the data indicate that only a few interactions deviate from those expected in a linear hierarchy (McGrew, 1972; Strayer and Strayer, 1976).

Another uniform trend is that most studies by ethologists have been static. That is, in the great majority, studies have described a given hierarchy structure at some particular time rather than explaining how that hierarchy structure was established or examining the processes by which members of the group changed rank over time.

The Human Social Science Approach

The research of sociologists and social psychologists, like that of ethologists, has provided, for the most part, static descriptions of social structure in small groups. There are a few notable exceptions (such as Newcomb's [1961] work) but these tend to utilize self-reported preference (friendship) data rather than observational data on asymmetric relationships. These static descriptions indicate a strong hierarchical component in the social structure of a broad spectrum of human small groups. Three areas of research are of relevance here: the study of human small groups in laboratory settings, the study of these groups in "natural" situations and the analysis of sociometric data.

When groups of unacquainted individuals are assembled in laboratory settings, a differentiation of members quickly emerges along such dimensions as frequency of originating and receiving various kinds of behavioral acts and ratings of leadership and likeability by fellow group members. (See Collins and Raven [1969], Gibb [1969], and Hare [1976] for comprehensive reviews.) Some members show behavioral profiles that give them relatively high control over the actions of their fellows and over group activities in general, while other members exert relatively little influence on either group activities or their colleagues (for example, see Bales and Slater, 1955, and the reviews cited above). Researchers using the status expectation paradigm have shown that external status characteristics—such as social class, race, and gender—influence the distribution of participation and prestige in these groups. (See Berger et al. [1972] for a general statement of the paradigm and Fennell et al. [1978] for a provocative discussion of differences in male and female groups.)

Although ethologists and laboratory small-groups researchers frequently collect the same kinds of data—individual A directs an act of type X to individual B—their analyses of the data are different. As mentioned above, ethologists look at the hierarchy structures produced by all possible pair-wise relationships among group members. Laboratory small-groups researchers, however, tend to concentrate on rank measures—the comparison of individuals in terms of total interaction rates or group preference scores. Bales et al. (1951) is a partial exception in that they give pair-wise interaction frequencies for eighteen aggregated sessions of six-man groups.

Studies in natural settings—such as those by Blau (1955) of a bureaucratic agency, Hanfmann (1935) of kindergarten children, Homans (1950) of an industrial work group and Whyte (1955) of gangs—provide further confirmation of the hierarchical structure of human small groups. These studies all find clearly differentiated status rank systems based upon both the behavioral actions and sentiments of group members. Although most of these studies, like the laboratory small-groups studies, do not provide data on all possible pair-wise relationships in their groups, the work of Hanfmann (1935) is an exception. Her data indicate the presence of a near-linear hierarchy in kindergarten children, comparable to those reported by ethologists for other human and animal groups. (See Mazur [1973] for a pioneering comparison of hierarchies in humans and animals; his approach and conclusions, however, differ from those presented here.)

The studies of sociometric data by Davis (1970), Hallinan (1974) and Holland and Leinhardt (1970; 1971; 1972) provide some of the most sophisticated descriptions available of social structure in small human groups. Although one might expect preference choices to yield structures considerably different from those produced by dominance relationships, there are in fact considerable similarities. These researchers have discovered (with high consistency across studies and samples) that there is a strong trend toward transitivity in the preference relations of group members (for example, if *A* chooses *B* as a friend and *B* chooses *C*, then *A* will choose *C* also). As will be explained in greater detail, there is a similar strong trend toward transitivity in the dominance relationships of human and animal groups. In a linear hierarchy all possible triads have transitive dominance relationships and in a near-linear hierarchy almost all the possible triads have transitive relationships. Davis (1970) suggests that, with more refined data where the stronger of the two preference relations for every pair in a group could be determined, "sociometric data would tend to fit the model of a transitive tournament" (p. 850). A transitive tournament is another term for a linear hierarchy and, if Davis' suggestion is correct, then social structures produced by properly refined preference relationships and dominance relationships would be identical.

THEORIES PROPOSED FOR THE EXPLANATION OF HIERARCHY STRUCTURES

I will now examine theories proposed—explicitly and implicitly—in both the animal behavior and human social sciences literature, to explain the formation of hierarchy structures. This examination is based upon previous research by the author (Chase, 1974). The procedure used in that study was that various theories of hierarchy structure were expressed in their basic (core) form, and that core form was converted into a mathematical model, a simple mathematical expression of what the core form implied. Then the stringency of the conditions needed by each mathematical model to predict the empirically common linear and near-linear hierarchies was examined and the available data inspected to determine if the conditions were met.

The two mathematical models that proved to encompass most of the explanations of hierarchies were a correlational model and a pair-wise interaction model. For example, explanations that are basically correlational models are those that indicate that individuals' positions in a hierarchy are determined by their physical attributes, their genetic endowment, their hormonal state, their past social performance, their personality traits, the social labels that they have been given or any composite of these factors. In order to account for linear and near-linear hierarchies, correlations between ranks in a hierarchy and their scores on any of the above-mentioned variables or composites would have to be .9 or greater (Chase, 1974). This theoretical result holds for linear and near-linear hierarchies no matter what species of animal, including humans, are involved and no matter what variables or composite of variables are used to predict rank in a hierarchy. This is a high correlation coefficient, indeed, and one which indicates that any correlational explanation must fulfill a stringent mathematical condition.

An examination of the literature indicates that correlations of .9 or higher are not usually found between a factor predicting dominance and rank in a hierarchy. Some of the best correlational data available are for animals and, specifically, for the premier animal of dominance studies—the chicken. Correlations vary in size for different investigations and, in studies that examined the association between an individual's aggressiveness—as indicated by its success in fights with other animals and its place in a hierarchy—correlations ranged from about .4 to .8 (Chase, 1974). These correlations, then, were not as high as the target value of .9, although some were near.

Explanations of hierarchies that are pair-wise interaction models in their canonical form are, for example, differences in fighting ability for animals, theories dealing with the interaction of personality types for humans and exchange theories for humans. In this model it is assumed that each member of a group has a pair-wise contest with each other member, that the winner of a contest dominates the loser in the group hierarchy and that an individual has a particular probability of success in each contest. This model requires that there must be one individual with a .95 probability of dominating each other individual, a second individual with a .95 probability of beating every one but the first individual and so forth down to the last individual who has only a .05 probability of beating any other individual (Chase, 1974). These results hold, regardless of the species of animal and regardless of what factors are assumed to explain success in pair-wise interactions. As in the correlational model, these results indicate that stringent mathematical conditions must be fulfilled with the pair-wise interaction model. Again, it has been found that data which best determined if these conditions were met were from animals, specifically chickens, and that the required conditions were *not* fulfilled (Chase, 1974).

It is not that correlational and pair-wise encounter theories and measurements give us no useful information about the success of individuals in dominance interactions or the places of individuals in hierarchies; they do, indeed, but the kind of information they give us is not sufficient to account for a group-level social structure, the overall hierarchy found in a group. Although individuals in a group may differ, it appears that the differences are not strong enough to explain empirically common dominance structures. (See Hallinan [1974] for a similar argument concerning individual differences and sociometric structures.)

TRIADS AND THE FORMATION OF HIERARCHIES

If many of the currently accepted theories of hierarchies and dominance relations are not adequate, then what might explain the presence of linear and near-linear hierarchies so frequently found in human and animal groups? As discussed above, theories that attempt to explain hierarchy structure by correlations (or the characteristics of single individuals) and theories that use pair-wise interactions (or the characteristics of pairs of individuals) appear to be inadequate. As Simmel realized long ago, three is a very important number in sociology, and I shall show that the structure of interaction in triads is very important for explaining the formation of linear and near-linear hierarchies. In order to understand the importance of triadic interaction, one must be aware of a simple mathematical fact: in a linear hierarchy all possible triads have transitive dominance relationships, and if a hierarchy is not linear, it contains at least one triad with an intransitive dominance relationship—and the fewer the intransitive triads, the closer the hierarchy to linearity. In a triad with a transitive dominance relationship, if individual A dominates B and B dominates C, then A also dominates C. So, A dominates the other two members, B dominates C, and C dominates no one. Figure 3.1A shows a triad with a transitive dominance relationship. In a triad with an intransitive dominance relationship, the

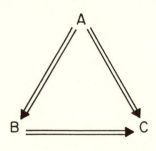

A. Transitive Triad   B. Intransitive Triad

Figure 3.1 Configuration of dominance relationships in a transitive and
an intransitive triad.

three individuals cannot be arranged in rank order because each
individual dominates one other individual. That is, A dominates,
say, B; B dominates C; and C dominates, rather than is dominated
by, A. Figure 3.1B shows a triad with an intransitive relation. In
a linear hierarchy all individuals can be ranked uniquely from
top to bottom by the number of group members they dominate,
and, therefore, any three can be ranked with respect to one another and form a transitive triad (this can be seen, for example,
by taking all possible subgroups of three in Table 3.1). In a hierarchy which is not linear, not all individuals are uniquely ranked
by the number of group members they dominate—there is at least
one tie and, therefore, at least one intransitive triad. Table 3.3
shows the dominance matrix for a group in which there is a tie
in rank between A, B and C and one intransitive triad involving
A, B and C.

Experimental Design and Data Collection

Could linear and near-linear hierarchies be so common because
animals and humans use behavioral processes which favor the
formation of transitive triads and discourage the formation of
intransitive triads? (Compare Davis [1970], Feld [1980], Hallinan
[1974] and Holland and Leinhardt [1970; 1971; 1972] for discussions of forces promoting transitivity in preference relationships.)
   In order to answer this question, I designed an experiment to

Table 3.3
Dominance Matrix Showing a Hierarchy with One Intransitive Triad Involving A, B and C

Dominant Animal	Dominated Animal					Number Dominated
	A	B	C	D	E	
A	--	1	0	1	1	3
B	0	--	1	1	1	3
C	1	0	--	1	1	3
D	0	0	0	--	1	1
E	0	0	0	0	--	0

determine the actual extent of transitive dominance relationships in groups of three individuals and, if transitivity were common, to discover the behavioral processes by which transitive relationships were generated. The species of choice for this experiment was the chicken; hierarchies in chickens are often linear or near linear as are hierarchies in more socially complex species such as primates and humans, but at the same time the behavior of chickens is simple enough so that it is more tractable to analysis. In addition, the most extensive dominance research on any species is on the chicken.

In this experiment, groups of three previously unacquainted chickens (all females) were placed in a neutral cage, and all aggressive actions among the individuals were recorded. Twenty-four triads were observed; each chicken took part in three triads, and each chicken in a group had been in the same number of triads previously. The data recorded consisted of the identity of the chicken initiating an aggressive action (the attacker), the identity of the chicken attacked (the receiver) and kind of aggressive action (peck, feather pull, claw (scratch), or jump on,) and the real (clock) time at which each attack occurred. Each triad was observed for four hours to give a grand total of ninety-six hours of observation time. A combined total of 2,801 aggressive acts

was recorded, and the resulting average rate of aggression was
29.2 acts per hour or 116.7 acts per triad.

An SSR keyboard was used to record the data. The data output
from the keyboard was converted to an electronic signal recorded
on audio tape with a standard tape recorder, and the resulting
data tapes were transcribed by computer to produce hard copies
of the data record and files for later analysis by computer. (See
Stephenson et al. [1975] and Stephenson [1979] for a description
of the SSR keyboard and its capabilities.) An excerpt from a data
record is presented in Table 3.4.

The Extent of Transitivity in Triads

When groups of previously unacquainted chickens are assembled, there are usually interchanges of aggressive actions between individuals although, in some pairs, one animal

Table 3.4
Data Excerpt

Act Number	Real Time	Time Interval	Aggressive Acts
0	09:30:25.1	---	Session Begins
1	09:31:01.8	36.7 sec.	3P1[a]
2	09:31:03.5	1.7	3P1
3	09:31:31.8	28.3	1P3
4	09:32:06.8	35.0	1P2
5	09:32:08.6	1.8	1PU2[b]
6	09:32:10.1	1.5	1C2[c]
7	09:32:14.9	4.8	3P1
8	09:32:18.6	3.7	1P2
9	09:32:21.2	2.6	3J2[d]

[a]"P" is the code for a peck.
[b]"PU" is the code for a feather pull.
[c]"C" is the code for a claw (scratch).
[d]"J" is the code for a jump on.

immediately submits to the other animal without ever fighting back. After either a short or more protracted series of interchanges, the asymmetric pattern of aggressive acts seen in established hierarchies develops: the interchanges stop and all or almost all of the aggressive actions are performed by one member of a pair against the other. At this point, one can think of a "decision" having been reached: a dominance relationship has been formed with one animal being dominant and the other subordinate.

In order to determine when a dominance relationship had been formed and, thus, to discover the extent of transitivity in the experimental triads, two criteria were used. One animal was considered to be dominant over another if: (1) it delivered any three aggressive actions in a row (any combination of pecks, feather pulls, jump ons, or claws) against the other animal and (2) there was a thirty-minute period, following the third aggressive act, during which the receiver of the aggression did not attack the initiator. The involvement of either member of the pair with the third member of a triad was not considered in these criteria and neither was the length of time necessary for the completion of the three acts. Once formed, a dominance relationship could be reversed if the subordinate animal fulfilled the criteria. While somewhat arbitrary, these criteria have support as a valid index of stable dominance relationships—of the fifty-four dominance relationships meeting the criteria in this study, only two were later reversed within the four-hour observation period (afterward, each chicken was returned to its home cage). The average time required to fulfill the criteria in the fifty-two initially formed relationships was 82.6 minutes, and only two relationships were established within less than thirty minutes before the end of an observation period. There was, then, a sufficient period after the formation of most relationships for reversals to occur.

An examination of the configuration of relationships at the end of each observation period indicated that one triad had no dominance relationships, seventeen had two and six had all three possible relationships. The seventeen triads with two dominance relationships all had the same configuration—one animal dominated each of the other two. If the two dominance relationships were determined randomly, this configuration would have a probability of .25 and would be expected to occur, by chance, about four times in seventeen. This configuration is shown in Figure 3.2A. It is important to note that this configuration guarantees a triad with transitive dominance relationships regardless of which subordinate later comes to dominate the other (preliminary analysis of data from several groups of four chickens each, observed for twelve hours, indicates that subordinate animals tend to form dominance relationships among themselves, in time). If B later dominates C, there is a transitive triad with A on top, B in the middle, and C on bottom. If C later dominates B, there is a transitive triad with A on top, C in the middle and B on the bottom.

Similarly, the six triads with three dominance relationships all had the same configuration, a triad with transitive relationships as shown in Figure 3.1A. A transitive triad has a probability of .75 of occurring if relationships are determined randomly—and would be expected to occur between four and five times out of six. Taken together, these findings demonstrate a marked tendency toward transitivity in the experimental triads, and this finding corroborates those of the studies of human and animal groups reviewed earlier.

An examination of the two groups with reversals in previously formed dominance relationships gives additional support for the

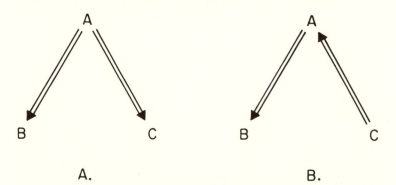

A.   B.

Figure 3.2 (A) Final configuration of dominance relationships in all triads having two extant dominance relationships at the end of the observation period. (B) Initial configuration of dominance relationships in triad with one reversal.

tendency toward transitivity. In one of these triads, animal *A* initially dominated *B* but was itself dominated by *C* (see Figure 3.2B). With this configuration an intransitive triad would have developed had *B* come to dominate *C* or a transitive triad if *C* had come to dominate *B*. In actual fact, *A* and *C* reversed their relationship and thus produced the configuration shown in Figure 3.2A, which guaranteed a transitive triad. In the other triad, the initial configuration of relationships was intransitive, as shown in Figure 3.1B. By the end of the observation period, *A* and *B* reversed their dominance, with the triad having the transitive relationship shown in Figure 3.1A resulting.

Behavioral Processes Leading to Transitivity

I now present a data analysis that shows how the interaction process in triads helps to explain the tendency toward transitive dominance relationships. The first part of the analysis treats the long-term structure of the interaction process and the second part, the short-term structure.

1. *Long-term Processes.* This analysis of long-term processes includes the seventeen triads with two relationships and the six with three relationships and excludes the one triad with no relationships. The analysis examines the effect of "winning" and "losing"—that is, the impact of either gaining dominance or becoming subordinate upon the further aggressive behavior of a chicken.

The analysis begins with the sixteen triads in which only two dominance relationships were formed (no reversals) and one triad with three relationships in which one animal first became dominant over the other two and then one of the subordinates became dominant over the other. (All other triads will be examined later.) An inspection of the first dominance relationship formed in each of the sixteen triads with two relationships reveals that there is one uniform pattern of behavior followed by each animal becoming dominant and another pattern followed by each animal becoming subordinate. The rule of strategy followed by each subordinate is to withdraw almost totally from all subsequent aggressive activity—not only against the animal that has become its superior but also against the bystander animal. None of the

sixteen animals becoming the first subordinate in these triads
ever became dominant over the bystander nor did any ever reverse its relationship with its superior. In addition, the rate of
aggressive activity of these animals dropped to almost zero after
they received the third attack from the chicken to which they
became subordinate; their average rate of aggressive activity before the third attack was 15.8 acts per hour, and after this attack
it was 0.2 acts per hour (significant at the $p < .02$ level, Wilcoxon
signed rank test). On the other hand, each chicken winning the
first dominance encounter went on to be aggressive toward the
bystander and to gain dominance over it.

There is a slight variation on these rules found in the single
triad in which one chicken first became dominant over the two
others and then one of the subordinates became dominant over
the other. In this triad, the strategy of the initially dominant
chicken was the same as in the preceding paragraph; it went on
to attack—and win dominance over—the bystander. The loser of
the initial dominance encounter, however, showed a small variation in strategy. After the third attack by the animal to which
it became initially subordinate, it initiated no aggressive acts at
all for 115 minutes; then it began to attack the bystander, later
winning dominance over it.

The next part of the analysis concentrates on four triads in
which three dominance relationships were formed. Figure 3.3
shows the order of formation of dominance relationships in these

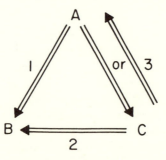

Figure 3.3 Configuration of dominance relationships in the transitive
triad resulting when the initial dominant and bystander engage in a dominance contest after each has won over the
initial subordinate.

triads. In these triads, the chicken losing the first dominance encounter lost a second dominance encounter with the by-stander, and, then, the animal who won the first dominance contest engaged the bystander (who had won the second dom-inance contest in the group) in a contest to determine dominance. The strategy of the initial subordinate was the same as in the groups above: it decreased its aggressive activity, and it did not become dominant over the bystander or reverse its relationship with its initial superior. The strategy taken by the winners in these triads is similar to that of the winners in the groups above; winners here directed aggressive acts toward the animal not yet dominated—that is, the winner of the initial contest and of the second contest (the bystander) battled for dominance. Initial dominators won over bystanders in three out of four cases, but no matter which won, a transitive triad was guaranteed by the initial configuration of relationships (A and C both dominated B).

The final collection of groups to be examined are the two triads in which an initially formed dominance relationship was later reversed. There were two extant dominance relationships at the end of the observation period in one of these triads and three relationships in the other. Figures 3.4A and 3.4B show the order of formation of relationships in these triads. In the group ending with two relationships, the initial subordinate became dominant over the bystander and then reversed its relationship with the

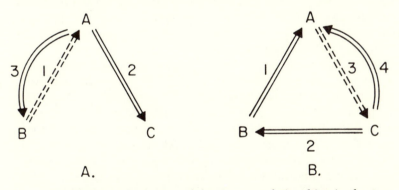

Figure 3.4 Order of formation of dominance relationships in the two triads with reversals (dominance relationships later reversed are indicated by dashed lines).

initially dominant chicken. The initial subordinate in this group did not follow the same strategy as losers of initial contests in the groups discussed above; it did not withdraw from aggressive activity. The winner of the initial contest also violated the usual strategy—it did not engage the bystander in a dominance contest. However, after the loser of the initial encounter became dominant over the bystander, it followed the usual winner's strategy of engaging the animal not yet dominated, and in this case the engagement resulted in a reversal.

In the group ending with three relationships, the initially dominant chicken was later dominated by the bystander, and the bystander was, in turn, dominated by the initially subordinate chicken. These relationships resulted in an intransitive triad until the bystander reversed its relationship with the initial subordinate to form a transitive triad lasting until the end of the observation period (see Figure 3.4B). In this triad, the bystander came to dominate the initial dominant rather than the initial subordinate as in the other triads in which the bystander forms a dominance relationship, the initially dominant chicken lost to the bystander (a rare event, it seems—based upon the data collected for this study, anyway) and the initial subordinate withdrew from aggressive activity only briefly and then won a dominance encounter against the bystander. At this point, each member of the triad was both a winner and a loser vis-a-vis the other triad members, and one of them (the bystander) followed a usual winner's strategy of engaging the animal not yet dominated; that engagement then resulted in a reversal and the formation of a triad with transitive relationships.

The usual strategies of both winners and losers (discovered here) help to explain the high proportion of triads with transitive relationships and triads guaranteed to be transitive. First, the withdrawal strategy of the initial subordinate guarantees that it will not be the dominant animal in the next relationship formed. Its withdrawal, therefore, obviates the possibility of a configuration of the type in which A dominates B and B dominates C. Without a configuration of this type there is no possibility for the formation of a triad with intransitive relationships (with a configuration of this type a transitive triad could still result, depending upon the direction of the third relationship). Second, the strategy of the initial winner—to engage the animal not yet dominated—guarantees the formation of at least two relationships in a triad. There are three subcases to be examined here. In the first subcase, the bystander does not win a dominance contest against either the initial subordinate or the initial dominant, and the initial dominant wins against the bystander. This results in a triad with a dominance configuration of the type in which *A* dominates both *C* and *B*, and such a triad is guaranteed to have transitive relationships, regardless of which of the subordinates later comes to dominate the other. In the second subcase, the bystander wins a dominance contest against the initial subordinate, and then both the initial dominant and the bystander follow the winner's strategy and engage in a dominance contest with each other. No matter which wins, a transitive triad will result; the transitivity is guaranteed by the configuration formed by the first two dominance relationships—*A* and *C* both dominate *B*. The third subcase is a residual collection in which, for example, a loser violates the usual strategy and wins against the bystander or a bystander wins against the original dominant in forming the second dominance relationship in a triad. In these situations, the eventual employment of the usual winner's strategy of engaging the animal not yet dominated can result in a reversal and a transitive configuration or a configuration which guarantees transitivity (see the analysis of the triads with reversals for examples).

2. *Short-term Processes.* Sequences of two successive aggressive actions can involve either just two, or all three, members of a triad. There are two possible kinds of sequences involving just two members: one animal attacks another twice in a row (Repeat sequence) or one animal attacks another and the receiver returns the attack (Interchange sequence). Act numbers 1 and 2 in the data excerpt given in Table 3.4 are an example of a Repeat sequence, and act numbers 2 and 3 are an example of an Interchange sequence.

These two pair-wise sequences, in contrast to the triadic sequences that will be defined below, have no implication, in and of themselves, for the formation of transitive or intransitive triads. Therefore, although the pair-wise sequences are interesting in their own right, the analysis here will concentrate on the triadic sequences.

There are four possible sequences involving all three members of a triad. At some point, one member of the triad attacks another member—almost without exception in experimental groups of chickens, attacks involve only two individuals at a time (the problem of coordinated attacks involving three or more individuals at a time, in such animals as primates, will be discussed later). The attacker in this encounter is labeled as *A*, the receiver as *B* and bystander as *C*. After *A* attacks *B* there are four *and only four* possible sequences involving *C*. *C* and *A* can interact, and there are two possibilities here: *A* can attack *C* or *C* can attack *A*. Or *C* and *B* can interact, and there are also two possiblities here: *C* can attack *B* or *B* can attack *C*. The resulting total of four possible sequences of attacks is shown in Figure 3.5. Pattern I is the Double

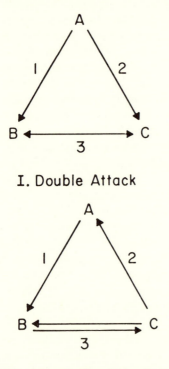
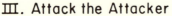

I. Double Attack

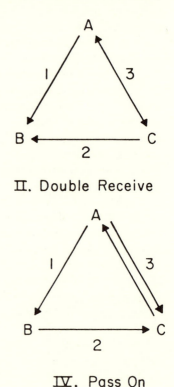

II. Double Receive

III. Attack the Attacker

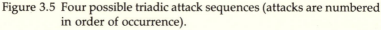

IV. Pass On

Figure 3.5 Four possible triadic attack sequences (attacks are numbered in order of occurrence).

Attack sequence: *A* first attacks *B* and then *A* follows with an attack on *C*. Pattern III is the Attack the Attacker sequence: *A* attacks *B* and then *A* is attacked by *C*. Pattern II is the Double Receive sequence: *A* attacks *B* and then *C* attacks *B*. Pattern IV is the Pass On (the Attack) sequence: *A* attacks *B* and then *B* attacks *C*. In the data excerpt of Table 3.4 act numbers 3 and 4 form a Double Attack sequence; act numbers 8 and 9, a Double Receive sequence; act numbers 7 and 8, a Pass On sequence; and act numbers 6 and 7, an Attack the Attacker sequence.

Two of these sequences have a different implication for the formation of transitive and intransitive triads based upon attack relationships than do the other two. (The reader should understand that transitivity and intransitivity are properties of relationships in general, not just of dominance relationships. Thus, if *A* dominates *B*, *B* dominates *C*, and *A* also dominates *C*, a transitive triad based on dominance relationships results; and if *A* attacks *B*, *B* attacks *C* and *A* also attacks *C*, a transitive triad based on attack relationships results.) Patterns I and II, the Double Attack and the Double Receive sequences, guarantee the presence of a triad with transitive attack relationships—no matter what the direction of attack in the third pair of the triad. This lack of dependency upon the attack in the third pair is indicated by the double-headed arrows in Figures 3.5I and 3.5II. For example, in the Double Attack sequence, if *B* later attacks *C*, the transitive triad in Figure 3.6A results; or if *C* later attacks *B*, the transitive triad in Figure 3.6B results. The problem of going from transitive triads based upon attack relationships to transitive triads based upon dominance relationships will be treated later.

In direct contrast, the Attack the Attacker and Pass On sequences can give rise to triads with either transitive or intransitive relationships, depending upon the direction of attack in the third pair. For example, in the Attack the Attacker sequence, if *C* attacks *B*, the transitive triad in Figure 3.7A results, but if *B* attacks *C*, the intransitive triad in 3.7B results. This dependency is signified by separate arrows in either direction for the third pair in Figures 3.5III and 3.5IV.

Given this difference in attack sequences, a question naturally arises: Are chickens favoring one or both of the sequences that guarantee transitivity over those not favoring transitivity? An

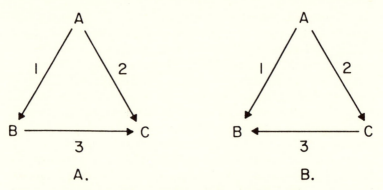

Figure 3.6 Two possible transitive triads resulting from a third attack following the use of a Double Attack sequence.

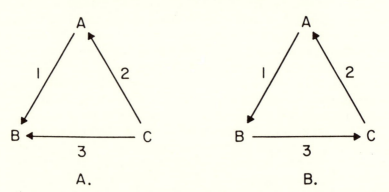

Figure 3.7 Possible transitive (A) and intransitive (B) triads resulting from a third attack following the use of an Attack the Attacker sequence.

analysis was performed to answer this question by determining the usage of the four triadic sequences. In this analysis, the first and second aggressive actions occurring in a triad were examined. If these two actions involved only two members of the triad, then the sequence was categorized as either a Repeat or an Interchange pattern as described above. If, however, the two actions involved first two members of the triad and then the third member, the sequence was categorized as one of the four triadic patterns. After comparing the first and second aggressive actions, the analysis continued by comparing the second and third actions, the third and fourth, and so on. As a result, in this method of analysis each action is considered once as the first act in a sequence and once as the second act. In addition, this method of analysis reidentifies the initial attacker, the initial receiver, and the bystander for each two-act sequence. Using this method of analysis on the data in Table 3.4, the first three sequences would be counted in this way: acts 1 and 2 are a Repeat sequence, acts 2 and 3 an Interchange sequence and acts 3 and 4 a Double Attack sequence.

Distribution of the four sequences as frequencies as well as percentages of all triadic sequences observed in twenty-three triads combined are given in Table 3.5. (One triad was omitted from this analysis; this triad had no incidences of triadic sequences and showed only a single Repeat pattern.) Column 6 of the table indicates the total usage of the four sequences not broken down by time between the initial and following acts of the sequence. The Double Attack sequence composes the overwhelming majority of all triadic patterns—86.6 percent. The Double Receive, Pass On, and Attack the Attacker sequences account for comparatively small percentages—2.7, 5.3, and 5.4, respectively—of all triadic patterns. If attacks are at random, each of the four patterns has an equal (.25) probability of occurring. The actual distribution of sequence patterns is, however, markedly different from that expected by chance (significant at the $p < .001$ level, using a multivariate normal test).

The finding that the Double Attack pattern comprises the large majority of all patterns is robust across sequences with different periods between initial and following acts. This can be seen by examining the first five columns of Table 3.5 in which sequences are broken down by the time, in seconds, between the initial and following acts. For the first four periods, the proportion of Double Attacks hovers around 90 percent, and in the longest period of separation, three-hundred seconds (five minutes) or more, the proportion drops somewhat to 76.8 percent.

The finding that most triadic sequences are Double Attacks is also robust across individual experimental groups. Of the twenty-four experimental triads, there were ten triads (41.7 percent of all triads) in which Double Attacks composed more than 90 percent of all sequences, four triads (16.7 percent) with between 80

Table 3.5
Percentage and Frequency Distribution of Triadic Sequences by
Time Interval between First and Second Acts (frequencies are in
parentheses)

	Time Interval (in sec.)					
Triadic Sequence	0–9.9	10.0–29.9	30.0–59.9	60.0–299.9	Over 300	Total
Double Attack	87.9 (123)	90.3 (102)	88.0 (73)	88.4 (137)	76.8 (76)	86.6 (511)
Double Receive	1.4 (2)	2.7 (3)	2.4 (2)	2.6 (4)	5.0 (5)	2.7 (16)
Pass On	7.1 (10)	.9 (1)	4.8 (4)	4.5 (7)	9.1 (9)	5.3 (31)
Attack the Attacker	3.6 (5)	6.2 (7)	4.8 (4)	4.5 (7)	9.9 (9)	5.4 (32)

percent and 89 percent Double Attacks, five triads (20.8 percent) with between 70 percent and 79 percent Double Attacks, and five triads (20.8 percent) with 43 percent or lower Double Attacks. (Considering the distribution of triadic sequences in each triad as a sample point, the vector of mean percentages for the patterns is significant at the $p < .001$ level, using a multivariate normal test.) In 79.2 percent of the triads, then, Double Attacks composed 70 percent or more of all triadic sequences, and the mean percentage of Double Attacks in the triads was 74.6 percent.

These data indicate that: (1) in most triads, most of the time, the chickens use the Double Attack pattern—a kind of sequence that guarantees triads with transitive attack relationships, and (2) in most triads, they only rarely use the Pass On and Attack the Attacker sequences that could possibly lead to intransitive triads. These findings suggest that the extremely high proportion of transitive triads and triads that are guaranteed to be transitive (one animal dominates the other two but the relationship between the subordinates is not settled), based on *dominance* relationships, results from the short-term interaction process of chickens in two ways. First, one chicken in a triad tends to repeatedly enact Double Attacks and, in so doing, fulfills the dominance criteria vis-à-vis the two other members of the group. Second, although chickens may on occasion use the Pass On and Attack the Attacker sequences, all three chickens in a triad do not enact these sequences in a sufficiently consistent and frequent manner so that dominance criteria over the animals being attacked are actually met. That is, in order to have a triad with intransitive *dominance* relationships there must be sufficient and consistent Pass Ons and/or Attack the Attackers to such a degree that a configuration of the sort in which *A* dominates *B* and *B* dominates *C* results *and*, further, sufficient and consistent Pass Ons and/or Attack the Attackers to such a degree that *C* comes to dominate *A*. Pass On and Attack the Attacker sequences are rare, to begin with, in most triads; and the few that do occur are not used consistently enough by the animals to meet the dominance criteria over their fellows in the proper pattern to form a triad with intransitive *dominance* relationships.

THE FORMATION OF LINEAR AND NEAR-LINEAR HIERARCHIES

I now present two empirically testable hypotheses based upon generalizations from the triad study. I propose that the hypotheses can help to direct research efforts and to explain the formation of linear and near-linear hierarchies—not only in groups of chickens larger than triads but also in other animal species and humans. (Data for some primate species will also be reviewed.) The first hypothesis originates from the long-term structure of the interaction process and the second from the short-term structure.

The first hypothesis is as follows:

A) The winner of a dominance contest tends to subsequently engage and dominate other individuals not yet dominated, but not individuals to which it is already subordinate;

B) The loser of a dominance contest tends not to attack any bystanders until the individual who has defeated it becomes dominant over the bystanders; and

C) If either or both of the two above conditions are violated, so that either a triad with intransitive dominance relationships or an initial configuration that could lead to an intransitive triad arises, then one individual will reverse an existing relationship in such a manner that a transitive triad or an initial configuration guaranteeing a transitive triad will result.

This necessarily somewhat complicated way of verbally stating the hypothesis simply implies that the initial configuration of dominance relationships (in most of the possible triads making up a large group) will be of the type in which A dominates both B and C or in which A and C both dominate B but not in which A dominates B and B dominates C. If either of the first two configurations is present, a triad is guaranteed to be transitive; and if all or most of the possible triads in a group have transitive dominance relationships or are guaranteed to be transitive, the hierarchy formed by the concatenation of the triads will be linear or near linear. One possible scenario of hierarchy formation arising from this hypothesis—and which I predict to occur very frequently—is as follows: One individual in a group wins successive dominance contests with all the other group members and each loser, in turn, withdraws from aggressive activity. After this first member has finished, one of the subordinates initiates and wins contests with all the other subordinates who again temporarily withdraw from aggressive activity. Then, a second of the original subordinates gains dominance over all but the initial dominant and the first subordinate and so on, until a complete linear hierarchy is established. In another likely scenario, two individuals each win one or more dominance contests with other group members. After this, the two winning individuals meet in a dominance encounter, and the winner goes on to dominate any remaining group members not yet dominated, while the loser withdraws temporarily from aggressive activity according to part B of the hypothesis. As indicated, intransitive triads and initial configurations that could lead to intransitive triads do arise when the usual strategies of winners and losers are not followed. Part C of the hypothesis suggests that (1) these structures are not as stable as actual transitive triads or configurations which guarantee transitivity, and (2) previously formed dominance relationships will be reversed to give transitive structures. Part C, in effect, indicates how individuals respond when there is an exception to parts A and B. Other researchers have also found that intransitive triads are not as stable as transitive ones in animals and tend to be converted to transitive structures (Murchison, 1935; Tordoff, 1972). Similarly, Hallinan (1974) and Holland and Leinhardt (1971) postulate that humans have a strong tendency to transform initially intransitive configurations of preference relations to transitive ones.

The second hypothesis states: The Double Attack pattern will be the most frequent of all sequences of two successive attacks involving more than two individuals. In other words, this hypothesis suggests that, of the four possible triadic sequences and the one possible tetradic sequence (A attacks B followed by C attacks D), the most frequent sequence will be the Double Attack pattern. If this hypothesis is supported, then most sequences that occur will generate configurations of attack relationships that guarantee transitivity, and those that generate configurations that do not guarantee transitivity will be rare. I would like to hedge (somewhat) my bet on this hypothesis by suggesting that in groups larger than three and which remain together for longer periods there might be a considerable occurrence of Double Receive sequences. This hedge is based upon preliminary observation of larger groups of chickens and on some data for primates which will be reviewed below. In some groups there is what might be called "scapegoating"—several members successively attack one low-ranking individual. These successive attacks on the "scapegoat" generate large numbers of Double Receive patterns. In any event, the Double Receive pattern, like the Double Attack, guarantees a transitive attack configuration, and either one or both patterns working together would help produce linear and near-linear hierarchies.

AGGRESSIVE SEQUENCES IN PRIMATES

The hypotheses presented above are derived from my own observational studies of chickens, and one might question the applicability of these hypotheses to other animal species and to humans. Are there indeed similar long- and short-term processes in the interactions of humans and other species that help to explain the reported prevalence of linear and near-linear hierarchies? As I mentioned earlier, animal behaviorists, sociologists, and social psychologists have provided relatively few studies of the dynamics by which hierarchies are formed. It is, therefore, not possible at the present time to rigorously test the validity of these hypotheses for human and other animal groups. There are, however, some suggestive reports in the primate literature and these shall now be reviewed. These studies give information about sequences of aggressive acts in primate groups with previously established relationships rather than sequences during the formation of dominance relationships as in the chicken experiment.[1] I have found no quantitative studies of the strategies used by winners and losers during the formation of relationships in primate groups.

Each of the four triadic sequences described has also been reported in various primate species. For example, the Double Receive sequence is reported in rhesus monkeys, Java monkeys, baboons, and langurs (Varley and Symmes, 1966; De Waal et al., 1976; Cheney, 1977; Hall and DeVore, 1965; Jay, 1965). Although the Double Attack sequence figures prominently in the results reported here, it has received relatively little recognition as an explicit sequence in primates (which is not to say that it is rare). It is, however, reported in Java monkeys, baboons, and langurs (De Waal et al., 1976; Hall and DeVore, 1965; Jay, 1965). The Pass On pattern is most recognized as an explicit sequence in primates, and it is referred to by a variety of terms including "redirected," "transferred," or "displaced" aggression. Pass On sequences are reported for rhesus monkeys, Java monkeys, and baboons (Altmann, 1962; Kaufmann, 1967; Jay, 1965; De Waal et al., 1976; Hall and DeVore, 1965). In some cases an animal attacked redirects the aggression to an inanimate object (Hall and DeVore, 1965). The Attack the Attacker sequence is frequently observed in primate groups when an individual aids a related animal being attacked, but it also occurs among nonrelated animals. This sequence is reported for pig-tailed monkeys, Java monkeys, and langurs (Tokuda and Jensen, 1968; De Waal et al., 1976; Jay, 1965).

Of these studies, only the one by De Waal et al. (1976) on Java monkeys, close cousins of the more familiar rhesus monkeys, reports the actual frequencies of occurrence of the four triadic sequence patterns.[2] Their study group was considerably different from those in my experiment; it consisted of seventeen animals of both sexes and of varying ages from infants to adults. The individuals had been together for a relatively long time, and it is probably safe to assume that most dominance relationships were firmly established rather than in the process of being formed. Their methods of counting triadic sequences were also different from those used in the chicken study. In order to count as a triadic sequence, A had to attack B and one of these two had to be involved in an attack with C less than fifteen seconds later. If the second attack took more than fifteen seconds, the interactions counted as separate dyadic attacks rather than as one triadic sequence.

Their data indicate that as proportions of all triadic sequences there were 39.7 percent Double Receives, 22.2 percent Double Attacks, 20.6 percent Pass Ons, and 17.5 percent Attack the Attackers (De Waal et al., 1976). In these data, the Double Receive patterns was used most frequently, with Double Attack a relatively distant second, followed closely by Pass On and Attack the Attacker. Although the Double Attack pattern does not make up the majority of all sequences in the Java monkeys as it did in the chickens, in both groups sequences which guarantee triads with transitive attack relationships are considerably more frequent than those which can lead to either transitive or intransitive triads. That is, the Double Receive and the Double Attack patterns, together, account for 61.9 percent, a majority of all triadic sequences in the monkeys. There is, then, agreement on the high proportion of sequences guaranteeing triads with transitive attack configurations between the experiment for chickens and one for a primate group under quite different conditions.

These data provide partial corroboration of the second hypothesis proposed above, but they also suggest certain refinements may be necessary for primates. Additional experiments under controlled conditions for both chickens and primates are required to ascertain the extent of the refinements. One necessary refinement concerns the presence of coalitions in primate groups. By coalition in this context I simply mean two or more individuals directing coordinated, interspersed aggressive acts toward another individual. Coalitions in primate groups are mainly of two sorts: (1) two or more animals join in attacking a third, and (2) one or more animals come to the defense of an animal being attacked and attack the original aggressor. These kinds of coalitions are commonly observed, for example, in baboons, rhesus monkeys, vervet monkeys, langurs, and Java monkeys (Cheney, 1977; Southwick et al., 1965; Varley and Symmes, 1966; Struhsaker, 1967; Jay, 1965; De Waal et al., 1976). The first kind of coalition can be considered as a modified type of Double Receive sequence; in this case the successive attacks are made by animals actively coordinating their aggressive actions. In a similar fashion, the second type of coalition can be considered as a variant of the Attack the Attacker sequence. Thus, the hypothesis proposed above concerning the short-term structure of aggressive interactions can be tested in socially complex species like humans and primates as well as in socially simpler animals using both the simple and modified forms of the triadic sequence patterns.

CONCLUSION

For both social scientists and animal behaviorists there are, arguably, three central issues in the study of social structure in small, face-to-face groups: formation, delineation, and consequence. Confronted with a small-group social structure, a researcher in either field might ask how the relationships came about, what the pattern of relationships was like, and what privileges or liabilities were associated with various positions in the structure. Both social scientists and animal behaviorists have made considerable progress with the last two of these issues, but neither group, as I have shown here through the example of hierarchy studies, has dealt satisfactorily with the formation of social structures. An analysis of the extant research demonstrates that common conceptual and methodological problems underlie the inadequacies of each field in dealing with the formation of hierarchy structures. Although it takes many different outward appearances, the conceptual machinery in both fields mainly tries to explain the formation of dominance hierarchies by differences in individual characteristics (including differences of ability in pair-wise encounters). Given this conceptual machinery, social scientists and animal behaviorists have developed a variety of sophisticated techniques to measure differences among individuals along a variety of dimensions. I have indicated here that, no matter how sophisticated the techniques of measurement or the models using individual differences, stringent mathematical conditions must be met before this approach can satisfactorily explain the empirically common linear and near-linear hierarchies. This emphasis on measuring things about individuals before they join a group, and correlating these measurements with their subsequent positions, leaves out what happens in between: the behavioral process by which individuals come to take their positions. Thus, the present theoretical approach in both human social sciences and animal behavior has led to a relative absence of empirical studies of the dynamics of hierarchy formation.

Herein, I offer a new and more satisfactory conceptual and methodological framework for the study of hierarchy formation. Here, the structure of the interaction process is seen as explaining the formation of a hierarchy, and the associated methodology deals with recording and analyzing the interactions among group members. Here, also, this approach is shown to view social structure as emerging from the web of interactions, and it naturally requires studies of the dynamic processes which result in hierarchy formation.

The application of this alternative approach led to the discovery of a short-term process, the predominant use of the Double Attack sequence, and a long-term process (usual patterns of behavior by winners and losers) that helped to explain the presence of actual transitive triads and configurations guaranteeing transitivity. These findings generated two hypotheses which proposed explanations for the presence of linear and near-linear hierarchies in animal and human small groups. A review of the primate literature offered partial support for one hypothesis, and it suggested modifications to make the hypothesis more generally applicable.

The results presented here suggest three major implications for future research on hierarchy formation, in particular—and on other kinds of social structures, in general.

The first implication is that the explicit and implicit assumptions made by explanations for the formation of various kinds of social structures should be critically examined. Other explanations based upon individual differences may also suffer from inherent liabilities similar to those for dominance hierarchies. This critical examination would, in appropriate circumstances, include explanations in both human social science and animal behavior. For example, profitable areas of investigation are likely to be wealth and income distribution in humans, resource distributions (mates, territories and so on) in animals and leadership and role structure in human small groups. (See Chase [1980] for a criticism of population genetics models as proximate explanations of cooperative and noncooperative behavior in animals.)

The second implication is that dynamic studies of dominance and other kinds of relationships can greatly increase our knowledge of small-group phenomena. The lack of such studies is partly explained, as discussed above, by the conceptual framework of present approaches and, partly, it seems likely, by the previous lack of efficient equipment for the recording, storage, and analysis of the necessarily large volumes of interactional data. The growing availability of microcomputer systems and computer-assisted devices for dealing with interactional data is rapidly alleviating this problem.

The third implication is that there is a certain "lawfulness" in the structure of interactions that can explain the configurations of social relationships in small groups. This article demonstrates "lawfulness" in the interactions of chickens in triads, and it goes on to suggest the units of interaction that are responsible for hierarchy formation in larger groups across species. The model developed here indicates how interactions at a microlevel—among individuals—can be cumulated to explain how a macrolevel structure—a dominance hierarchy—is produced.

I suggest that this kind of approach has applicability beyond hierarchy research to the study of other types of social structure in human and animal groups. Future research is needed to assess the validity of this implication.

NOTES

1. A particular aggressive sequence used during the formation of dominance relationships may have a different implication than the same sequence used after dominance relationships have been formed. For example, if A attacks B, and B passes on the attack to C, then there is at least a logical possibility that C might later attack A to form an intransitive triad if A does not already dominate C. On the other hand, if A already dominates both B and C and B dominates C, then the same Pass On sequence would not make an intransitive triad possible because C, in all probability, would not later attack A.

2. Although Kummer (1975) does not count frequencies of behavioral sequences, he does present a stimulating analysis which suggests that interactions in mixed-gender triads can help to explain dominance relationships and sexual alliances in larger groups.

REFERENCES

Altmann, S.A. A field study of the sociobiology of rhesus monkeys. *Ann. NY Acad. Sci.* 102:338-435, 1962.

Bales, R.F., and Slater, P.E. Role differentiation in small decision-making groups. In: *Family, Socialization and Interaction Process*. T. Parsons and R.F. Bales (Eds.), Free Press, New York, pp. 259-306, 1955.

Bales, R.F.; Strodtbeck, F.L.; Mills, T.M.; and Roseborough, M.E. Channels of communication in small groups. *Am. Soc. Rev.* 16:461-68, 1951.

Bekoff, M. Quantitative studies of three areas of classical ethology: Social dominance, behavioral taxonomy, and behavioral variability. In: *Quantitative Methods in the Study of Animal Behavior*. B.A. Hazlett (Ed.), Academic Press, New York, pp. 1-46, 1977.

Berger, J.; Cohen, B.P.; and Zelditch, M., Jr. Status characteristics and social interaction. *Am. Soc. Rev.* 37:24-255, 1972.

Brown, J.L. *The Evolution of Behavior*. W.W. Norton, New York, 1975.

Blau, P.M. *The Dynamics of Bureaucracy*. University of Chicago Press, Chicago, 1955.

Chase, I.D. Models of hierarchy formation in animal societies. *Behav. Sci. 19*:374-82, 1974.

Chase, I.D. Cooperative and noncooperative behavior in animals. *Am. Nat. 115*:827-857, 1980.

Cheney, D.L. The acquisition of rank and the development of reciprocal alliances among free-ranging immature baboons. *Behav. Ecol. Sociobiol. 2*:303-18, 1977.

Collins, B.E., and Raven, B.H. Group structure: Attraction, coalitions, communication, and power. In: *Handbook of Social Psychology*, 2d. ed. G. Lindzey and E. Aronson, (Eds.), Addison-Wesley, Reading, MA, pp. 102-204, 1969.

Davis, J.A. Clustering and hierarchy in interpersonal relations: Testing two graph theoretical models on 742 sociograms. *Am. Soc. Rev. 35*:843-52, 1970.

De Waal, F.B.M.; van Hoof, J.A.R.A.M.; and Netto, W.J. An ethological analysis of types of agonistic interaction in a captive group of Java-monkeys (*Macaca fascicularis*). *Primates 17*:257-90, 1976.

Feld, S. The structure of inequality in groups. Unpublished manuscript, Department of Sociology, SUNY, Stony Brook, NY, 1980.

Fennell, M.L.; Barchas, P.R.; Cohen, E.G.; McMahon, A.M.; and Hildebrand, P. An alternative perspective on sex differences in organizational settings: The process of legitimation. *Sex Roles 4*:589-604, 1978.

Gibb, C.A. Leadership. In: *Handbook of Social Psychology*, 2d ed. G. Lindzey and C. Aronson (Eds.), Addison-Wesley, Reading, MA, pp. 205-82, 1969.

Guhl, A.M. Social behavior of the domestic fowl. In: *Social Hierarchy and Dominance*. M. Schein (Ed.), Dowden, Hutchinson and Ross, Stroudsberg, PA, pp. 156-201, 1975.

Hall, K.R.L., and DeVore, I. Baboon social behavior. In: *Primate Behavior*. I. DeVore (Ed.), Holt, Rinehart and Winston, New York, pp. 53-110, 1965.

Hallinan, M.J. *The Structure of Positive Sentiment*. Elsevier, Amsterdam, 1974.

Hanfmann, E. Social structure of a group of kindergarten children. *Am. J. Orthopsychiatry 5*:407-10, 1935.

Hare, A.P. *Handbook of Small Group Research*, 2d ed. Free Press, New York, 1976.

Hausfater, G. Dominance and reproduction in baboons. *Contributions to Primatology*, vol. 7. Karger, Basel, 1975.

Holland, P.W., and Leinhardt, S. A method for detecting structure in sociometric data. *Am. J. Soc, 76:*492-513, 1970.

Holland, P.W., and Leinhardt, S. Transitivity in structural models of small groups. *Comp. Group Studies 2:*107-124, 1971.

Holland, P.W. and Leinhardt, S. Some evidence on the transitivity of positive interpersonal sentiments. *Am. J. Soc. 77:*1205-9, 1972.

Homans, G.C. *The Human Group.* Harcourt, Brace and World, New York, 1950.

Jay, P. The common langur of North India. In: *Primate Behavior.* I. DeVore (Ed.), Holt, Rinehart and Winston, New York, pp. 197-249, 1965.

Jolly, A. *The Evolution of Primate Behavior.* Macmillan, New York, 1972.

Kaufmann, J.H. Social relations of adult males in a free-ranging band of rhesus monkeys. In: *Social Communication among Primates.* S.A. Altman (Ed.), University of Chicago Press, Chicago, pp. 73-98, 1967.

Kummer, H. Rules of dyad and group formation among captive gelada baboons (*Theropithecus gelada*). In: *Proceedings of the Symposia of the Fifth Congress of the International Primate Society.* Japan Science Press, Tokyo, pp. 129-59, 1975.

McGrew, W.C. *An Ethological Study of Children's Behavior.* Academic Press, New York, 1972.

McHugh, T. Social behavior of the American buffalo (*Bison bison bison*). In: *Social Hierarchy and Dominance.* M. Schein (Ed.), Dowden, Hutchinson and Ross, Stroudsberg, PA, pp. 213-21, 1975.

Marler, P. Studies of fighting in chaffinches (1) Behaviour in relation to the social hierarchy. *Br. J. Anim. Behav. 3:*111-17, 1955.

Mazur, A. A cross-species comparison of status in small established groups. *Am. Soc. Rev. 38:*513-30, 1973.

Missakian, E.A. Aggression and dominance relations in peer groups of children 6-45 months of age. Paper presented at the annual meeting of the Animal Behavior Society, Boulder, CO, 1976.

Murchison, C. The experimental measurement of a social hierarchy in *Gallus domesticus:* IV. Loss of body weight under conditions of mild starvation as a function of social dominance. *J. Gen. Psychol. 12:*296-312, 1935.

Newcomb, T.M. *The Acquaintance Process.* Holt, Rinehart and Winston, New York, 1961.

Sade, D.S. Determinants of dominance in a group of free-ranging rhesus monkeys. In: *Social Communication among Primates.* S.A. Altman (Ed.), University of Chicago Press, Chicago, pp. 99-114, 1967.

Savin-Williams, R.C. Dominance in a human adolescent group. *Anim. Behav. 25:*400-6, 1977.

Savin-Williams, R.C. Dominance hierarchies in groups of early adolescents. *Child Devel.* 50:923-35, 1979.

Savin-Williams, R.C. Dominance hierarchies in groups of middle to late adolescent males. *J. Youth Adolescence* 9:75-85, 1980.

Schein, M.W., and Fohrman, M.H. Social dominance relationships in a herd of dairy cattle. *Br. J. Anim. Behav.* 3:45-55, 1955.

Southwick, C.H.; Beg, M.A.; and Liddiqi, M.R. Rhesus monkeys in North India. In: *Primate Behavior.* I. DeVore (Ed.), Holt, Rinehart and Winston, New York, pp. 111-59, 1965.

Strayer, F.F., and Strayer, J. An ethological analysis of social agonism and dominance relations among preschool children. *Child Devel.* 47:980-89, 1976.

Stephenson, G.R. PLEXYN: A computer-compatible grammar for coding complex social interactions. In: *Social Interaction Analysis.* M.E. Lamb, S.J. Suomi and G.R. Stephenson (Eds.), University of Wisconsin Press, Madison, pp. 157-84, 1979.

Stephenson, G.R.; Smith, D.P.; and Roberts, T.W. The SSR system: An open format event recording system with computerized transcription. *Behav. Res. Meth. Instru.* 7:497-515, 1975.

Struhsaker, T.T. Social structure among vervet monkeys (*Cercopithecus aethiops*). *Behaviour* 29:83-121, 1967.

Tokuda, K., and Jensen, G.D. The leader's role in controlling aggressive behavior in a monkey group. *Primates* 9:319-22, 1968.

Tordoff, H.B. Social organization and behavior in a flock of captive, non-breeding red crossbills. *Condor* 56:346-58, 1954.

Tyler, S. J. The behaviour and social organization of the New Forest ponies. *Anim. Behav. Monogr.* 5:87-196, 1972.

Varley, M., and Symmes, D. The hierarchy of dominance in a group of macaques. *Behaviour* 27:54-75, 1966.

Whyte, W.F. *Street Corner Society*, 2d ed. University of Chicago Press, Chicago, 1955.

Wilson, E.O. *The Insect Societies.* Belknap Press of Harvard University Press, Cambridge, 1971.

Wilson, E.O. *Sociobiology: The New Synthesis.* Belknap Press of Harvard University Press, Cambridge, 1975.

4

Emergent Hierarchical Relationships in Rhesus Macaques: An Application of Chase's Model

Patricia R. Barchas and Sally P. Mendoza

There are no two individuals of any given species which, when living together, do not know which of the two has precedence and which is subordinate.
—Schjelderup-Ebbe (1935; p. 949)

Schjelderup-Ebbe's pioneering work with birds has provided primatology, for better or worse, with its conception of dominance relations. Research completed since Schjelderup-Ebbe's description of dominance-subordinance relations has qualified the application of the dominance concept (Rowell, 1974; Coe and Rosenblum, in press), however, there has been little revision of the concept itself. Dominance is generally viewed as the outcome of a competitive encounter where the prize for the contest winner is prerogative to pursue desired incentives without interference from the loser.

One of the contributions Schjelderup-Ebbe made to subsequent investigators of dominance is the implicit assumption that dominance relations are dyadic. Even Allee, one of the champions of group influence on individual behavior, views dominance relationships "as a real expression of crude, person-against-person competition for social status and they furnish fair illustrations of the individualistic egocentric phase of group biology" (Allee, 1943; p. 517). This concept of individual-against-individual competition is reiterated in modern literature (Jones, 1981; Popp and DeVore, 1979). Given this implicit aspect of dominance relationships, it is indeed surprising that dominance hierarchies are often used as a measure of social organization of primate groups. According to Schjelderup-Ebbe and others since (Clutton-Brock and Harvey, 1976; Popp and DeVore, 1979; Rowell, 1974), the appearance of a hierarchical structure is merely a convenient shorthand for observers which aids in the organization of data but is not a behavioral reality for the group members.

In the preceding chapter, Ivan Chase presented an analysis of group formation in chickens which seemingly contradicts the notion that dyadic dominance resolutions proceed without constraint from the larger group structure. Quite the contrary, his work suggests that status resolutions among dyads proceed in such a way that an ordered linear hierarchy at the group level is generally insured. In short, this work suggests that the resultant group structure is as important in determining the course of dyadic resolutions as are the actors themselves. Chase's argument, if it can be substantiated, clearly represents an important departure in the study of dominance relationships.

It is the purpose of this chapter to examine social interactions displayed in newly formed triads of rhesus macaques to determine whether or not the processes delineated by Chase can be detected in a nonhuman primate species. The impact of relationship formation on other behavioral dynamics involved in group formation will also be assessed. Furthermore, since this method does represent a departure from traditional modes of conceptualizing status relationships and status hierarchies, it will provide a basis for re-examination of other basic tenets and assumptions previously employed in the study of dominance.

SUBJECTS AND METHODS

Subjects for this study consisted of twenty-seven female and twelve male rhesus macaques (*Macaca mulatta*). The monkeys were a part of a transient population held by Woodard Asiatic, San

Francisco, for quarantine purposes between capture in India and distribution to research centers in the United States. All subjects were imported two to six weeks prior to data collection and were judged to be fully mature.

Prior to testing, subjects were assigned to within-sex triads with members of a given group carefully matched for external characteristics which may influence the formation of status relationships such as size, age, general activity levels and reproductive state. The animals were handled, evaluated, and matched by an experienced veterinarian. Subjects were housed apart from each other in individual guillotine cages until twenty minutes prior to observation, at which time the monkeys were moved in their cages to the test room. The cages were visually separated from one another by opaque dividers minimizing interanimal communication but allowing nominal habituation to test the environment. Following this habituation period, guillotine doors to the individual cages were simultaneously raised allowing the monkeys to emerge from their individual cages into the larger testing room. (For methodological details, see Barchas [1971].) Interactions which ensued were recorded on audio tape by a single observer viewing the monkeys through a window positioned such that all parts of the room were continuously visible to the observer. For each interaction, the observer recorded the initiator, the recipient, and the type of behavior according to a prespecified list of behaviors (Chance, 1956). Transcription of behavioral events preserved the sequence and time to the nearest minute of interactions.

Behaviors of relevance to this presentation may be categorized as: *Dominance* behaviors, including attack, threat, stare, mount and displace; *Submissive* behaviors, including fear grimace, present for mount, and avoid; *Affiliative* behaviors, including grooming, huddling and sitting in close proximity; and *Investigative* behaviors, including visual, manual or olfactory exploration. In addition, two behaviors which are considered important to establishment of spacing within a group were also examined: *Approach* and *Move Away*.

RESULTS

The first finding of significance was that all monkeys did, in fact, emerge from their holding cages. The initial behaviors which typically followed release of the monkeys primarily consisted of exploratory behaviors of both the environment and each other. There was a notable absence of overt aggression in the initial encounters. This suggests that either the opportunity to interact with conspecifics or the lure of greater freedom of movement overcame any expression of xenophobia which often accompanies encounters of strangers of this species (Southwick *et al.*, 1974).

Temporal Order of Relationship Formation

Fairly soon after the initial encounters, subjects began to exhibit signs of dominance or deference. In order to determine whether a dominance relationship was established, an arbitrary criterion was used: two successive dominance acts initiated by one individual and received by another separated by no more than two minutes and followed by five minutes in which the recipient of the initial interactions did not reciprocate with any dominance gesture nor did the initiator direct any submissive gestures to the recipient. Similar criteria were used to indicate a relationship established by way of submissive gestures. In this case, two submissive behaviors directed by one animal toward another within a two-minute period followed by five minutes during which the order suggested by the initial acts were not reversed in either dominance or submissive acts. These criteria are substantially different from those used by Chase. However, reduction in the time required to achieve criteria in this study was essential to allow time for reversals to occur and increased the probability that such reversals would occur.

The results of this analysis have been previously reported (Mendoza and Barchas, in press) and may be summarized as follows: In the thirteen groups observed, there were thirty-nine dyads. Of these, thirty-four achieved the criteria indicating the relative status of dyad members was determined. Mean time to completion of status resolution was 13.9 minutes. No dyad reversed the initial status determination despite the fact that there was ample time remaining during the test period for reversals to have occurred. In twelve of the thirteen groups observed in this study, at least two of the dyadic status relationships were resolved within the forty-five minute test period. Examination of the temporal order in which these relationships were formed revealed that linear hierarchies were insured upon resolution of status in the second dyad in each of the twelve groups.

Behaviors by Phase of Relationship Formation

By designating the actual time during which criteria are achieved, it is possible to delineate three phases of relationship formation: *before* status determination, *during* status determination, and *after* status determination. In order to examine the impact of phase of relationship formation on the patterns of interaction for behaviors other than dominance and submissive behaviors, the frequency occurrence per minute was determined for each dyad. Behaviors were further categorized by status of the initiator and status of the recipient of the interaction. Analyses were performed for each sex with a 2 (status) X 3 (phase) analysis of variance with repeated measures on the last factor.

Investigative behaviors showed a significant decrease across phases for females (F (2, 80) = 5.87, $p < .01$). The males showed a similar pattern of interaction across phases, although the differences did not achieve statistical significance (see Figure 4.1A). This suggests that, particularly prior to relationship formation, the group members engage extensively in social evaluation behaviors which may be important in monitoring not only other individuals but interactions between other dyads.

Males showed the highest frequency of Affiliative interactions before relationships were established (F (2, 36) = 4.01, $p < .05$), did not interact affiliatively during relationship formation, and only infrequently after relationship formation (see Figure 4.1B). In comparison to males, females showed a relatively high level of affiliative behavior and this rate of interaction was maintained across phases.

The behaviors primarily related to increasing or decreasing social distance, Approach and Move Away, were also impacted by resolution of status relationships. Both dominant males and females showed a higher frequency of Approach toward subordinates than the subordinates toward the dominants (F (1, 18) = 7.60, $p < .05$ and F (1, 40) = 4.46, $p < .05$, respectively, see Figure 4.2a), indicating that the dominant members of the dyad were

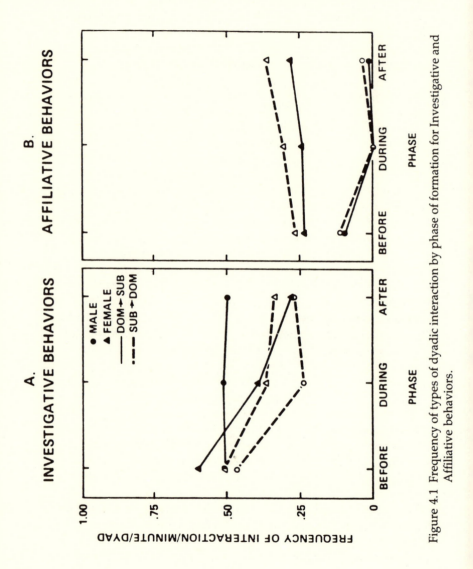

Figure 4.1 Frequency of types of dyadic interaction by phase of formation for Investigative and Affiliative behaviors.

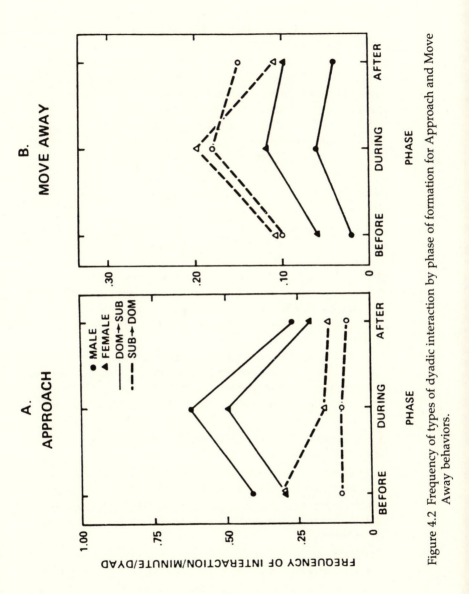

Figure 4.2 Frequency of types of dyadic interaction by phase of formation for Approach and Move Away behaviors.

87

responsible for decreasing social distance more often. Since the males were already differentiated on this behavior prior to relationship formation, it may be important to examine this more closely as a possible cue to outcome of initial status interactions. During relationship formation, both dominant and subordinate females attempt to increase social distance as shown by the significantly higher frequency of Move Away for the during phase ($F (2, 80) = 6.03, p < .01$, see Figure 4.2b). The frequency of Move Away for males was not significantly impacted by either phase of relationship formation or status.

Sequential Analysis of Dyadic Analysis

The preceding sections of this chapter have suggested that dyadic dominance relationships are formed with the resultant structure "in mind." The next step is to examine the sequence of dyadic interactions to determine whether or not constraints exist on the patterning of interactions between members of a triad which would tend to insure interactions consistent with a particular social organization—in this case, a linear dominance hierarchy.

This analysis is the same as that described by Chase in the previous chapter for examination of short-term processes leading to linear dominance hierarchies. Briefly, sequences of the interactions were categorized according to whether they followed:

(1) *Repeat Pattern*, where animal A initiated two successive acts to the same recipient, B;

(2) *Reversal Pattern*, where animal A directed an act to animal B, and the next interaction of that type was initiated by B and directed to A;

(3) *Double Initiate Pattern*, where animal A directed a behavior toward B and the next behavior of that type was initiated by A to the other group member, C;

(4) *Double Receive Pattern*, where animal A initiated a behavior toward B and the next behavior of that type was initiated by C toward B;

(5) *Initiator Receives Pattern*, where the first act initiated by A and received by B is followed by animal C initiating the same type of behavior with A receiving the act;

(6) *Pass-on Pattern*, where animal B, the recipient of the first act initiated by A, initiates the second act directed toward C.

After all possible sequences of behaviors of a given type were categorized according to the above scheme, results were subjected to a chi-square analysis to determine whether or not sequences involving three animals followed the Double Initiate or Double Receive pattern (consistent with formation of only linear relations) more often than the Initiator Receives or the Pass On patterns (consistent with either linear or nonlinear relations). Results from each behavioral category were analyzed separately for male groups and female groups. While not included in the analyses, the frequency with which sequential acts followed the Repeat or Reversal patterns are included in the table for comparative purposes.

Dominance interactions in the male groups followed the Double Receive pattern significantly more often than any of the other three patterns of sequential interaction ($\chi^2 = 96.06$, $p < .001$; see Table 4.1). Females showed more frequent use in their dominance interactions of the patterns consistent with linear hierarchies although this effect was not significant ($\chi^2 = 7.22$, $p < .10$). This lack of significance may be primarily attributable to the overall diminished frequency of dominance interactions in female groups as compared to that occurring in male groups.

For subordinance interactions (see Table 4.1) both males and females followed patterns consistent with linear relationships ($\chi^2 = 40.25$, $p < .001$ and $\chi^2 = 45.19$, $p < .001$, respectively) and for both sexes the Double Initiate pattern occurred with the greater frequency than the Double Receive pattern.

It was of interest to determine whether or not other behavioral interactions, not directly related to assessment of status relationships, also follow this sequential patterning. For this purpose, Grooming and Investigative behaviors were also analyzed. These behaviors were selected because, like the Dominance and Submissive behaviors, identification of initiator and recipient within a given dyad is highly reliable, in contrast to behaviors like Sit Near, where it is often difficult to determine which of two animals is the intended recipient.

Females showed predominantly the Double Receive pattern of

Table 4.1

Categorization of Sequential Interactions Given an Initial Act $A \rightarrow B$

		Repeat $\underline{A} \triangleright \underline{B}$	Reverse $\underline{B} \triangleright \underline{A}$	Double Initiate $\underline{A} \triangleright \underline{C}$	Double Receive $\underline{C} \triangleright \underline{B}$	Initiate to Initiator $\underline{C} \triangleright \underline{A}$	Pass On $\underline{B} \triangleright \underline{C}$
Dominance	Male	35.5	2.8	3.8	17.8	2.5	3.0
	Female	11.3	0.4	2.0	2.7	1.3	1.3
Subordinance	Male	46.8	1.0	12.8	5.8	2.0	2.0
	Female	20.3	0.6	9.9	4.3	1.9	1.2
Investigative	Male	23.0	14.5	23.0	23.0	15.5	13.0
	Female	23.2	13.8	21.9	26.5	13.7	11.0
Grooming	Male	3.8	.3	0.0	0.0	0.0	.3
	Female	15.9	1.8	0.8	4.7	1.3	1.4

Note: All figures expressed as $\bar{x}$ frequency of occurrence per group.

interactions for Grooming ($\chi^2 = 40.92$, $p < .001$). Males did not engage in this behavior with sufficient frequency to permit analysis. For Investigative behaviors, both sexes interacted most frequently in accordance with the Double Receive and Double Initiate patterns ($\chi^2 = 14.53$, $p < .01$; and $\chi^2 = 104.63$, $p < .001$, respectively), and for both sexes Double Initiate occurred more frequently than either of the remaining patterns. It should be noted that the ordering of successive acts can be consistent with linear relationships without the total pattern of interactions indicating hierarchical relationships or indeed even differential rates of interaction between dyad members. Thus, these data do not indicate that Grooming and Investigative behaviors are initiated by some animals and received by others, nor do the data speak to whether or not status influences the expression of these behaviors. What the data do suggest is that there exists constraints at the group level which influences which dyadic interactions are likely to occur at any given time.

Chase's Hypothesis Confirmed

The data presented above indicate that Chase's hypothesis is viable when applied to a primate species, *Macaca mulatta*. Following introduction of previously unfamiliar animals, dyadic relationships were formed in a temporal order which insured that linear hierarchies would emerge.

While the criteria for detecting that status differentiation within a dyad had been accomplished were arbitrary, there are indications that the measurements employed were nonetheless meaningful. That is, no reversals of the initial determination were observed, even though ample time remained allowing for the possibility of reversals. Furthermore, other behaviors not believed to be involved in the establishment of hierarchies were impacted by phase of relationship formation. For the female groups, Investigative behaviors were higher before relationship formation and Move Away occurred with the greatest frequency during relationship formation. Similarly, for males, Affiliative Interactions disappeared completely during relationship formation and only partially reemerged following relationship formation. Thus, the phase demarcated by achievement of criteria, while arbitrarily defined, did seem to represent a shift in the orientation of dyadic members to each other.

In addition to the Dominance and Submissive behaviors, the frequency with which animals Approach one another was also influenced by relative status. Dominant animals initiate Approach more often than subordinate animals. For females, this differential rate of Approach initiation did not appear prior to relationship formation. Dominant males, however, already showed greater frequencies of Approach than did subordinate males prior to the time that the criteria employed indicated that differential status was determined. This suggests for males, on at least this behavioral dimension, that either relative status was already determined prior to the during phase or that this behavior may act as a cue for subsequent resolution of relative status. As noted above, the three phases of relationship formation can be distinguished behaviorally not only with respect to Dominance and Submissive behaviors but by other behavioral categories as well. By this argument, the latter possiblity thus seems more likely, but since the effect was only apparent among the males tested, closer examination of this behavior during group formations needs to be completed before either possibility should be accepted or rejected.

Sequential analysis of behavior provides perhaps the most convincing evidence that factors at the group level play a considerable role in regulating dyadic interactions. Group members interacted predominantly in ways that were consistent with linear patterns and inconsistent with potentially nonlinear patterns. Which of the two patterns consistent with linear interactions were employed most often appears to be a function of the specific behavioral pattern examined. That is, sequences of submissive behaviors followed the Double Initiate pattern more often than the Double Receive pattern whereas Dominance Investigative and female Grooming followed the Double Receive pattern more frequently than the Double Initiate pattern. For each of the behavioral patterns subjected to this analysis, with the exception of Grooming, the Double Initiate and Double Receive patterns of interaction occurred with greater frequency than either the Initiate to the Initiator or the Pass On patterns.

The Investigative behaviors require a special note. For this behavior there does not appear to be an overall difference in the frequency of Initiation according to status. That is, interactions are as frequently initiated by dominant animals as by subordinate animals (see Figure 4.1A). Nevertheless, examination of sequential acts, as noted above, reveals that this behavior is constrained in temporal expression in a manner consistent with linear relations. This suggests that there is more than one dimension involved in the processes leading to linear dominance hierarchies and clearly justifies Chase's separation of the short-term and long-term aspects of this problem.

DISCUSSION

These data lend further confirmation to Chase's hypothesis that animals interact in a way that is consistent with linear relationships. For both species tested, chickens and rhesus macaques, the prevalence of strong linear hierarchies has been repeatedly reported as a central feature of the social organization found among groups of the species. For the rhesus macaque groups contained in this study, the patterning of interaction was not restricted to dominance and submissive behaviors but was apparent in other types of interactions as well. Thus, the patterning of interactions which ensue following introduction of previously unfamiliar animals appears to be constrained, insuring the emergence of the species-typic pattern of social organization.

Implications for Understanding the Concept of Dominance

The most notable impact Chase's method of analysis has for our conceptualization of dominance relationships is the strong implication of involvement of social organization in regulating dyadic encounters. It is difficult to conceptualize dominance as being a one-to-one contest with winner take all, when the very interactions which presumably decide the contest are constrained by group considerations. Other data from this study, presented previously, also argue against the view that dominance relations are resolved by way of dyadic contests (Mendoza and Barchas, 1983). Relationships are formed too rapidly and with a notable absence of agonistic encounters prior to the establishment of directionality of status within the dyads for such a view to be tenable. Furthermore, individual characteristics were controlled in this study by matching group members as closely as possible for age, size, sex, reproductive state and activity levels. Since these factors should act to facilitate resolution of dominance relationships, a struggle for dominance, if it were to take place, should have been heightened in this study. The group formations could not be characterized as a struggle or even a contest, indicating that a revision in our conceptualization of status relationships is necessary.

The dominant animal's behavior in this study appears to be as restricted by social considerations as is the subordinate's behavior. Thus, the idea of an unrestrained alpha animal and an inhibited gamma animal must also be reconsidered. The only incentive clearly present in this study is incentive to interact socially. In pursuit of this goal, both dominant and subordinate animals act within the constraints of the social order. Dominance relationships, then, do not emerge only with respect to priority of access considerations as has recently been argued (Popp and DeVore, 1979).

Finally, the idea that socialization (Hall, 1965) and social observation (Rowell, 1974) are critical to one animal learning his status with respect to another does not receive support from this study. Both the rapidity of relationship formation and the constancy with which it is upheld argue against relationships being formed by either method. This is not to say that either socialization or social observation does not play major roles in primate behavior. Indeed, they must. Animals not fully socialized are not able to form stable relationships as adults nor are they able to act in accordance with the relationships between others (Anderson and Mason, 1978). Furthermore, social observation seems to be a critical factor in explaining the manner in which interactions were found to be sequenced in this study. These processes do not, however, explain the resolution within a dyad of which animal is to become dominant and which is to become subordinate.

With the introduction of Chase's insights into the dominance literature, reconsideration of previously held tenets becomes absolutely essential. Schjelderup-Ebbe's long-standing description of dominance relations, their underlying motivations and impact on the social life of animals, as reflected in the quote at the beginning of this chapter, must finally be revised. The exact form of the revision is beyond the scope of the present chapter but it must come to view dominance relations as a unit of group organization in which individual goals, incentives and benefits assume a secondary position to social organization and group cohesiveness.

REFERENCES

Anderson, C.O., and Mason, W.A. Competitive social strategies in groups of deprived and experienced rhesus monkeys. *Dev. Psychobiol. 11*: 289-99, 1978.
Allee, W.C. Where angels fear to tread: A contribution from general sociology to human ethics. *Science 97*:517-25, 1943.

Barchas, P.R. Differentiation and stability of dominance and deference orders in rhesus monkeys. Ph.D. dissertation. Stanford University, 1971.

Chance, M.R.A. Social structure of a colony of *Macaca mulatta*. *Br. J. Anim. Behav.* 4:1-13, 1956.

Clutton-Brock, T.H. and Harvey, P.H. Evolutionary rules and primate societies. In: *Growing Points in Ethology*. P.P.G. Bateson and R.A. Hinde (Eds.), Cambridge University Press, Cambridge, MA, pp. 195-238, 1976.

Coe, C.L., and Rosenblum, L.A. Male dominance in the bonnet macaque:A malleable relationship. In: *Social Cohesion: Essays Toward a Sociophysiological Perspective*. P.R. Barchas and S.P. Mendoza (Eds.), Greenwood Press, Westport, CT, in press.

Hall, K.R.L. Aggression in monkey and ape societies. In: *Primates: Studies in Adaptation and Variability*. P.C. Jay (Ed.), Holt, Rinehart and Winston, New York, pp. 149-61, 1965.

Jones, C.B. The evolution and socioecology of dominance in primate groups: A theoretical formulation, classification and assessment. *Primates* 22:70-83, 1981.

Mendoza, S.P., and Barchas, P.R. Behavioral processes leading to linear status hierarchies following group formation in rhesus macaques. *J. Human Evol.* 12:185-92, 1983.

Popp, J.L., and DeVore, I. Aggressive competition and social dominance theory: Synopsis. In: *The Great Apes*. D.A. Hamburg and E.R. McCown (Eds.), Benjamin/Cummings Publishing Co., Menlo Park, CA, pp. 317-40, 1979.

Rowell, T.E. The concept of social dominance. *Behav. Biol.* 11:131-54, 1974.

Schjelderup-Ebbe, T. Social behavior of birds. In: *A Handbook of Social Psychology*. C. Murchison (Ed.), Clark University Press, Worcester, MA, pp. 947-73, 1935.

Southwick, C.H.; Siddiqui, M.F.; Farooqui, M.; and Pal, B.C. Xenophobia among free-ranging rhesus groups in India. In: *Primate Aggression, Territoriality and Xenophobia*. R.L. Holloway (Ed.), Academic Press, New York, pp. 185-210, 1974.

5

From Pair-Wise Dominance Relations to Dominance Relations in Small Groups: A Test of a Graph Theoretic Model

Henry A. Walker

INTRODUCTION

Several chapters in this volume discuss dominance relations using information about social processes in animal groups to make inferences about social processes in human groups. The problem of predicting dominance orders in animal groups has intrigued students of animal behavior for well over a generation. In this chapter a model generated from a theory of human behavior is applied to animal groups in order to predict dominance rank.

The use of a model generated from human sociological theory to explain or predict animal behavior is justified on a number of grounds. First, many animals live in social groups similar to those in which humans live and work. Much of the social behavior which those animals exhibit is as complex as that exhibited by their human counterparts.

Second, many of the social behaviors and processes extant in animal groups are apparently highly similar to behaviors and processes found in human groups. Specifically, dominance relations in animal groups seem strikingly similar to power and influence relations in human groups. For example, both influence and dominance appear to be relations rather than attributes of individuals. Neither dominant (or subordinate) humans nor animals are always dominant (or subordinate). Hence, one individual may dominate two others in one context, be subordinate to one and superordinate to the other in another context or be subordinate to a coalition of the two in a third context.

Third, although the sociological theory of power discussed in this chapter (Emerson, 1962, 1972a, 1972b; Walker, 1977) addresses some issues which are not of central concern, the model which is generated is designed to apply to issues in human processes. Thus, while the argument presented here should not be construed as a test of the theory, it does provide a test of fit of the application of the model.

Dominance and Power: Two Puzzles

Dominance relations have been observed among a variety of animal species and have been described in considerable detail. Although the determinants of dominance position, as well as the behaviors through which dominance is exhibited appear to vary among species, there are some regularities. Among these regularities it may be noted that stable dominance relations are typically linear and although triangular relations are observed, they appear to be unstable, are often marked by conflict and tend to be replaced by linear patterns. A persistent problem for students of animal behavior has been their inability to predict dominance relations in a group from knowledge of the paired interactions of group members outside the group context. In addition, it is unclear how triangular relations are related to the linear relations which so often replace them. Intransitive triangular relations or tournaments of the form, $A \rightarrow B$, $B \rightarrow C$, $C \rightarrow A$, do occur in groups which exhibit patterns of dominance and deference. However, triangular relations appear to be unstable and generally resolve to strictly linear hierarchies (Murchison, 1935).

Power relations in human groups appear similar in many ways to dominance relations in animal groups. For example, there are a number of determinants of power and of influence and the behaviors through which power is manifested are varied and complex. Although power is not logically transitive, observations suggest that power relations, like dominance relations in animal groups, tend to result in linear influence relations.

It is not clear to students of human behavior how or if dyadic power relations combine to form power relations in triads and larger groups or if different organizing principles operate in the larger groups. Thus the concern of sociologists to specify more clearly the determinants of power and of influence relations in triads and larger groups parallels the concern of their counterparts to determine the relation of pair-wise dominance relations to dominance relations in larger animal groups.

Dominance Relations

A dominance order has been defined as "the set of sustained aggressive-submissive relations" (Wilson, 1975; p. 279). However, the use of the term "aggressive" may be misleading since stable animal groups are generally characterized by low levels of conflict and aggression. Indeed, it has been argued that one function of dominance orders is the establishment and maintenance of peaceful group relations (Hinde, 1974). Jolly (1972) has suggested that other terms including *status* may be more appropriate.

Dominance relations have been observed across a range of vertebrate and invertebrate animal species since the pioneering studies of dominance relations among vertebrates of Schjelderup-Ebbe (1935). Although Wilson's definition of dominance suggests that the best indicator of dominance may be the outcome of agonistic encounters, a number of other indicators have been used, including priority of access to incentives, for example, food, territory and sex, and grooming behavior.

There appear to be a number of determinants of pair-wise dominance in animals including size, age, gender and kinship. However, the correlations of these factors with dominance rank in groups are often low or moderate at best. There is convincing evidence, especially from among some primate species, that dominance relations are socially created and maintained (cf. Bernstein and Mason, 1963; Mason, 1961). Animals use a variety of gestures and social cues which suggest their dominance rank, and the addition, loss or replacement of one animal can result in significant reorganization of a group's dominance order.

Maslow (1936) noted that the dominance orders in groups of macaques could not be determined from knowledge of the paired interactions of group members outside the group context. That is, if two animals have an established "peck order" in which A dominates or influences B and those animals are introduced into a larger group, B may dominate A in the order which is established in the group. This observation has been sustained over years of investigation under both natural and controlled conditions. This suggests that characteristics of the social situation may have important effects on the establishment and maintenance of dominance orders.

Power and Influence in Human Groups

Weber (1947) defines power as "the probability that one actor within a social relationship will be in a position to carry out his own will despite resistance" (p. 247). There are a number of determinants of power including size, physical attractiveness and control of scarce resources. Power is manifest in human groups by priority of access to incentives and through influence on behavior, that is, by the capability of one group member to get another member to do something he would not otherwise do or alternatively *not* to do something he would otherwise do (cf. Dahl, 1957; Bachrach and Baratz, 1970).

Although many students of power relations argue that power is a conception applicable to triads and larger groups, the language of power typically is the language of dyadic relations. With some notable exceptions, for example, Shapley and Shubik (1954), measures of power are dyadic and it is difficult to apply existing theories of power to triads and larger groups. However, human interaction is not confined to a series of dyadic relations. Such a restricted conception of the world severely constrains our understanding of how power works. In the next section of this essay, I will describe how this difficulty is overcome in one theory of power—the theory of power and dependence relations (Emerson, 1962, 1972a, 1972b). In that section, a model is developed which allows the theory to be tested in triads and larger groups.

Power-Dependence Relations

The theory of power and dependence relations suggests that the power of an actor A over another B (P_{ab}) is determined by the mutual dependence of A on B and of B on A (D_{ab} and D_{ba}, respectively). The dependence of B on A varies directly with motivational investment, the extent to which B desires something which A possesses or controls, and inversely with the availability of alternative sources of that which A possesses. The amount of influence which can potentially be realized in any power-dependence relation is equal to B's dependence on A minus A's dependence on B. This relation can be expressed as shown in equation (5.1).[1]

$$P_{ab} = D_{ba} - D_{ab} \qquad (5.1)$$

Equation (5.1) quantifies both the P_{ab} and P_{ba} relations. If (5.1) is used to calculate P_{ba} it follows that P_{ba} is negative when P_{ab} is positive and $P_{ab} = P_{ba}$ in just the case that D_{ab} and D_{ba} are equal. If P_{ab} is zero, A and B have equal dependence on one another and power is said to be balanced (Emerson, 1962). If this is the case, neither A nor B can influence the other. If P_{ab} is nonzero and positive, A can dominate B, that is, power imbalance exists.

While this conception of power appears relatively simple and is intuitively appealing, it has not been useful for discussing power in triads and larger groups for at least two reasons.[2] First, equation (5.1) has no counterpart in groups in which N is greater than 2. Second, although Emerson's use of the term "balance" has some intuitive meaning in dyads, that is, power is in a sense counterbalanced, neither the meaning of balance nor the relation of balance to power is clear in triads or larger groups.

A Revised Formulation and a Model

In the simplest case of relations in a triad, that is, a system in which A and B and B and C are linked by relations of mutual dependence, a determination of the hierarchy of power would appear to be relatively straightforward. If A is more powerful than B and B is more powerful than C it would seem that A can influence C indirectly, through B. Thus, the arrangement $A > B$

> C would appear to be reasonable. However, this arrangement depends on the absence of a direct A-C relation.

If a direct A-C relation exists and A has more power than C, the hierarchy of power, once again, would appear nonproblematic. The question is, can this relatively simple relation be meaningfully represented in the manner of equation (5.1) above? If the logic of (5.1) is applied, statements (5.2, 5.3, 5.4) must be factual.

$D_{ab} < D_{ba}$ (dependence of A on B is less than dependence of
$\quad\quad\quad$ B on A)   (5.2)

$D_{bc} < D_{cb}$ (dependence of B on C is less than dependence of
$\quad\quad\quad$ C on B)   (5.3)

$D_{ac} < D_{ca}$ (dependence of A on C is less than dependence of
$\quad\quad\quad$ C on A)   (5.4)

Each of the three statements is a statement about dyadic relations. None of the three statements suggests how one dyadic relation is affected by the existence of the other two relations. The importance of this observation is clearer when the case in which no group member dominates any other group member is examined.

The situation in which no pair-wise relation outside the group context is nonzero is the situation in which equations (5.5), (5.6) and (5.7) are statements of fact.

$$P_{ab} = D_{ba} - D_{ab} = 0 \quad\quad\quad\quad (5.5)$$
$$P_{bc} = D_{cb} - D_{bc} = 0 \quad\quad\quad\quad (5.6)$$
$$P_{ac} = D_{ca} - D_{ac} = 0 \quad\quad\quad\quad (5.7)$$

Each of those statements represents an example of the kind of situation which Emerson referred to as balanced. Yet in the three-actor case it is possible for each of these statements to be true while the statement, $D_{ba} \neq D_{ca}$, is also true. This possibility raises a number of questions. Is it the case that no group member can influence any other members in this situation? Is the situation balanced? How are the pair-wise relations represented by equations (5.5), (5.6) and (5.7) related to the structure of group relations, that is, the set of relations formed by aggregating the paired relations? The answers to each of these questions is ambiguous in the theory of power-dependence relations. In order to answer those questions in a meaningful sense, it is necessary to generalize the conception of power and dependence relations to triads and larger groups.

Power and Group Structure

The central issue of this section is whether pair-wise interactions observed outside the group context provide information useful to a determination of dominance relations in the group and if the information is used, how it is used. It has been pointed out that power and dominance relations are characteristics of groups rather than of group members. The mathematical theory of graphs has been utilized to clarify issues related to the structure and dynamics of groups (Berge, 1962; Flament, 1963; Harary, Norman and Cartwright, 1965). In the graphic representations which follow, group members or social objects (A, B, . . . , N) are represented as points of a graph while relations among group members (R_1, R_2, . . . , R_N) are represented as signed, directed lines.

Power has been defined as a relation of relative dependence among actors. For any pair of actors the less dependent member of the pair is the more powerful. Relations of relative dependence are formally defined as follows:

DEFINITION 1. *An actor A has low dependence (R_1) relative to another actor B if A's dependence on B is less than or equal to B's dependence on A.*

DEFINITION 2. *An actor A has high dependence (R_2) relative to another actor B if A's dependence on B is greater than B's dependence on A.*

These definitions can be applied to dyads and graphs constructed by assigning positive valences to low dependence relations (actors with low dependence have positive power or influence potential) and negative valences to high dependence relations. Figure 5.1 represents the set of all possible dyadic relations.

One characteristic of graphic structures like those in Figure 5.1 is balance (Flament, 1963). Harary (1953-54) has proved a number of theorems about balance. For example, a graphic structure is

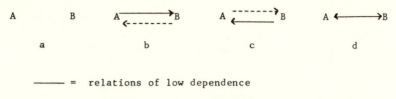

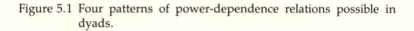

Figure 5.1 Four patterns of power-dependence relations possible in dyads.

balanced if (1) every semicycle of the graph is positive, (2) for every pair of points, every semipath joining them has the same sign or (3) the points of the graph can be partitioned into two mutually exclusive subsets such that each positive path joins a pair of points in the same subset and each negative path joins a pair of points from different subsets. While these criteria are structurally equivalent, they are all incorporated in a formal definition of balance.

DEFINITION 3. *A graph is* balanced *if (1) every semicycle of the graph is positive, (2) for every pair of points, every semipath joining them has the same sign or (3) the points of the graph can be partitioned into two mutually exclusive subsets such that each positive path joins a pair of points in the same subset and each negative path joins a pair of points from different subsets.*

The terms used in definition 3 can be illustrated using the graphic structures in Figure 5.1. Each signed, directed line between points in Figures 5.1b, 5.1c and 5.1d is a *path*. The length of a path is the number of lines making up the path. Thus each figure, with the exception of 5.1a, has two paths of length one and one path of length two or two-path. Paths in which not all subpaths run in the same direction are *semipaths*. Thus the directed path *ABA* is a semipath. Closed paths or semipaths are *cycles* (or semicycles). Hence, the dyad is a special case in which every two-path is a semicycle of length two. Finally, the *valence* of a path is determined by the product of the signs of the lines making up the path. Thus, Figure 5.1b has a positive path from *A* to *B*, a negative path from *B* to *A* and one negative semicycle.

Application of the criteria specified in definition 3 to Figure

5.1b indicates that the graph is not balanced. The unique semi-cycle is negative rather than positive. In addition, since A and B are joined by both a positive and negative path, it is obvious that the two points cannot be members of the same *and* different sub-sets. Similar application of these criteria to all the graphs in Figure 5.1 indicates that only Figure 5.1d is balanced. This figure represents the case which Emerson described as balanced—the case in which $D_{ba} = D_{ba}$.[3] Thus, the Emersonian example of balance is consistent with the graphic definition of balance. It would appear that balance in the graph theoretic sense is related to balance of power and dependence, at least in the dyadic case. However, graph theoretic balance is a characteristic of all signed, directed graphs. The utility of the conception for students of power-de-pendence relations depends on developing a meaningful defi-nition of balance of power-dependence relations in triads and larger groups—a definition which is consistent with balance in the graph theoretic sense.

Figure 5.2 suggests some dependence relations which are pos-sible in the triad. Each of the graphs in Figure 5.2 contains three semicycles of length two and eight semicycles of length three. If Harary's criteria of balance are applied to the graphs depicted in Figure 5.2 only one graph, Figure 5.2c (the graph in which all pair-wise dependencies are equal), is balanced. The other three figures and the systems of power-dependence relations which they represent are unbalanced.

Figure 5.2 is also important for what it does not indicate. Figure

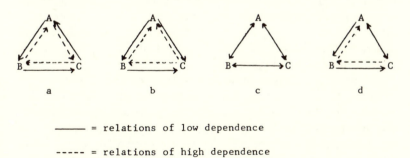

a   b   c   d

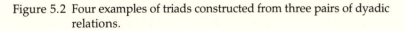

———— = relations of low dependence

- - - - - = relations of high dependence

Figure 5.2 Four examples of triads constructed from three pairs of dyadic relations.

5.2a is a triangular relation and the power-dependence order of the group cannot be readily determined. Figure 5.2d is a variant of Figure 5.2a in which no clear pattern of dominance obtains in a pair A——C. Again, the nature of power-dependence relations in the group is not clear. Figure 5.2b represents a linear hierarchy. Thus, while a graphic representation of power-dependence relations may provide a means of determining which groups have hierarchical structures—depending on whether they are balanced or not—it is not possible to determine on inspection where group members rank in groups which have hierarchies if triangular relations or balanced pair-wise relations exist. Resolution of this problem requires some measure which uniquely represents the power and dependence of each group member relative to every other member.

Local Balance and Degrees of Balance

If balance is related to absence of hierarchy, the question arises, "Do groups become less balanced as the hierarchy approaches strict linearity?" A measure which indicates the degree to which a structure is unbalanced would appear to be important in answering that question.

A number of measures which describe the degree to which both graphs and points of a graph are balanced have been proposed. These measures of *structural* and *local* balance do not uniquely differentiate social structures such as those depicted in Figure 5.2. (See Taylor [1970] for a review of balance measures.) For example, the structures depicted by Figures 5.2a and 5.2b differ in only one respect—the nature of the two-cycle which describes the A——C relation. The signs of the paths in Figure 5.2a are reversed in Figure 5.2b.

I propose a measure of structural balance and a measure of local balance in order to differentiate structures like those depicted by Figures 5.2a and 5.2b and the points of those structures. The measures take the following information into account: (1) The presence or absence of direct dependence relations between every member of the group and every other member, (2) the presence or absence of indirect relations between each group member and every other member, (3) the strength of indirect relations (treated as a function of length of connecting paths) and (4) valences of relations.

It is assumed that pair-wise relations and the nature (valence) of those pair-wise relations are important in determining influence (dominance) in groups. In addition, it is assumed that the relation of each group member to any other group member is influenced by their pair-wise relation and each of their relations with every other group member, the extent to which those relations are direct or indirect and the character (valence) of those relations. As a simplifying assumption, it is assumed that addition of group members does not alter the basic dependence relations between pairs of actors although additions may affect influence (dominance) relations which are related to dependence. Based on these assumptions, the two measures of balance I propose utilize the ratio of the number of shortest positive paths between points to the total number of shortest paths in a graphic structure with paths weighted as a function of path length. Paths which are comprised solely of positive (low dependence) relations are treated as positive paths. All other paths are negative. The structural balance measure is calculated from (5.8) while the measure of local balance, that is, the balance of a point, is calculated from (5.9).

$$B(G) \; = \; \frac{\sum_i \sum_j P^+_{ij}{}^{(1/l)}}{\sum_i \sum_j P_{ij}{}^{(1/l)}} \tag{5.8}$$

$$B(i) \; = \; \frac{\sum_j P^+_{ij}{}^{(1/l)}}{\sum_j P_{ij}{}^{(1/l)}} \tag{5.9}$$

Equations (5.8) and (5.9) can be applied to any signed, directed graph, G, in which i and j are points in G; l is the length of a path and P^+_{ij} and P_{ij} are the number of shortest positive paths and shortest paths from i to j in G.

Calculating Structural and Local Balance

The number of paths in graphs of power-dependence relations may be counted in graphs with four or fewer points. In larger structures it is useful to use matrix methods. A reachability matrix for low dependence and for high dependence relations can be constructed by entering 1 at each ij if j is reachable from i by that relation and 0 if the relation is absent. The reachability matrix for low dependence relations, R_1, is raised to successive powers until D, the matrix which results when all j are reachable from all i or j is not reachable from i, is obtained. Subsequent to this operation, the matrix R_2 is raised to D and $B(G)$ and $B(I)$ are calculated.

The balance measures theoretically vary from 0 to 1. The measure of structural balance is equal to 0 if a graph contains no low dependence relations, while it is equal to 1 in instances in which a graph contains no high dependence relations. The measure of local balance, $B(I)$, also varies from 0 to 1. The measure is equal to 0 when all relations emanating from a point, I, are relations of high dependence and is equal to 1 when all relations emanating from a point are relations of low dependence.[4]

Interpreting Balance Measures

The measure of local balance is the key to interpreting the balance "profile" of a graph and the group it represents. Because the measure is an indicator of the proportion of an actor's relations, which are relations of low dependence, differences in balance measures are indicators of the relative dependence of actors to the group (all actors taken into account). As a consequence, actor A, who has low dependence relative to actor B when only pair-wise relations are examined, may be dominated by B in a group context if A has high dependence relations with every other group member while B has low dependence relations with every other group member. The measure of local balance uniquely differentiates points in Figures 5.2b and 5.2d but does not differentiate points in either Figure 5.2a or 5.2c (see Table 5.1).

Examination of the pair-wise relations in Figure 5.2b suggests that point B is dominated by point A, while point C is dominated by both A and B. The expected order of dominance is $A \to B \to C$. This represents strict hierarchy. The measures of local balance for points A, B and C are 1.00, .50 and .00. Hence, if this measure mirrors relative dependence in the group context, an assignment of dominance based on the balance measure is consistent with the assignment based on intuition.

Table 5.1
Measures of Structural and Local Balance for Digraphs of Four Triads

MEASURE OF BALANCE	TRIAD DEPICTED IN FIGURE 5.2			
	a	b	c	d
B(G)[a]	.500	.500	1.000	.667
B(A)[b]	.500	1.000	1.000	1.000
B(B)[b]	.500	.500	1.000	.600
B(C)[b]	.500	.000	1.000	.500

[a]Measure of structural balance
[b]Measure of local balance

Figure 5.2d has the same order of local balance as that in Figure 5.2b. The measures of local balance for points A, B and C are 1.00, .60 and .50, respectively. Thus, an interpretation of dominance relations based on the balance measure results in an assignment identical to the assignment suggested for Figure 5.2b. However, the magnitudes of the measures suggests that the differences in relative dependence of points B and C is less in Figure 5.2d than in Figure 5.2b.

The balance measures for structures 5.2a and 5.2c are similar in that measures of local balance do not differentiate points within structures. However, both structural balance measures and measures of local balance vary across structures. Figure 5.2c has a measure of structural balance which is 1.00, as does each point in the figure. No point has an advantage over any other point. The structure would appear to be the triadic counterpart of what Emerson referred to as a balanced case.

On the other hand, Figure 5.2a represents an instance of a triangular system of relations in which every member can potentially influence every other member (albeit in some cases only indirectly). From the perspective of group structure, each group member stands in a similar relation to every other group member. The measures of local balance suggest that there is no clear order of dominance in the group. Thus, rankings based on the measure of local balance for both of these structures coincide with and provide an approximation of rankings of power and influence or dominance. The measures of structural balance suggest that Figure 5.2a more nearly approximates the hierarchy than Figure 5.2c. In the next section, the measure of local balance is utilized to predict relations in larger group structures from knowledge of pair-wise relations formed outside the group context.

Predicting Dominance Relations from Pair-wise Data

It is assumed that the measures derived above are useful for predicting the relations of group members from knowledge of pair-wise relations established outside the group context. In this section the measure of local balance will be applied to (1) hypothetical data to demonstrate its utility as an aid in more clearly specifying group structures and (2) data taken as reported from studies of dominance relations in rhesus macaques (*Macaca mulatta*). In the latter application the fit of the model is evaluated by examining the Spearman correlation coefficient of the dominance rank of group members, predicted from the measure of local balance, to the actual rank assigned by trained observers.

Application 1. Landau (1951) noted the existence of the relation of the score structure of a group and the presence or absence of hierarchy in the group. The score structure, V, of a group represents the set of numbers which specifies the number of group members dominated by each group member. Landau noted that the score structures of two groups may be the same even though the groups have different internal structures. The matrices in Table 5.2 illustrate the problem.

The matrices represent dominance relations for each ij as follows: If i dominates j, 1 is entered at ij in the matrix and -1 is entered at ji. These entries correspond to positive directed lines (low dependence relations) and negative directed lines (high dependence relations), respectively. The distance matrix, the matrix which results when the basic matrix is raised to successive powers such that each point i is reachable by a series of positive paths from every other point j or i is not reachable by positive paths from j, is 2 for matrix one and 3 for matrix two. The score struc-

Table 5.2
Matrices Representing Relations among Members of Two Groups Which Have the Same Score Structures but Different Internal Structures of Relations

$$
M_1 = \begin{array}{rrrrr}
0 & 1 & 1 & 1 & -1 \\
-1 & 0 & -1 & 1 & 1 \\
-1 & 1 & 0 & -1 & 1 \\
-1 & -1 & 1 & 0 & 1 \\
1 & -1 & -1 & -1 & 0
\end{array}
\qquad
M_2 = \begin{array}{rrrrr}
0 & 1 & 1 & -1 & 1 \\
-1 & 0 & 1 & 1 & -1 \\
-1 & -1 & 0 & 1 & 1 \\
1 & -1 & -1 & 0 & 1 \\
-1 & 1 & -1 & -1 & 0
\end{array}
$$

Adapted from Landau (1951).

Table 5.3
Measures of Structural and Local Balance for Two Five-Member Groups

	GROUP I		GROUP 2
MEMBER	MEASURE OF LOCAL BALANCE	MEMBER	MEASURE OF LOCAL BALANCE
1	.818	1	.800
2	.600	2	.636
3	.600	3	.600
4	.600	4	.636
5	.500	5	.437
B(G) = .615		B(G) = .620	

Adapted from Landau (1951)

tures of the two groups, $V = (3, 2, 2, 2, 1)$, are the same although the patterns of dominance relations within the group, that is, pair-wise relations, differ. The effects of those differences may be illustrated by using the measure of local balance (see Table 5.3).

The measures of structural balance for matrices one and two are .615 and .620, respectively. The ratio of shortest positive paths to total number of shortest paths is slightly greater for the group represented by matrix two. It is the comparison of measures of local balance which is most instructive. Using the measures to predict group structure from pair-wise data results in two quite different predictions. Group 1 is predicted to have a dominance order of $1 > 2 = 3 = 4 > 5$, while the dominance order in group 2 is predicted to be $1 > 2 = 4 > 3 > 5$. Thus, even though the score structures are the same, interpretations of the measures of local balance suggest somewhat different group structures. In one instance the measure of local balance predicts dominance relations which are consistent with predictions which could be made from the score structures alone, but in the second case the predictions based on the measures of local balance are not consistent with predictions based on the score structure. These differences result because the measure of local balance takes into account both the number of group members dominated and the relation of group members to one another.

Application 2. Varley and Symmes (1966) studied various features of the dominance hierarchy of a captive colony of rhesus macaques over a period of ten months. The colony consisted of two male and four female animals who were under observation for a period exceeding fifteen months. After the group established a stable dominance hierarchy, a series of pair-wise dominance tests and tests of dominance in larger groups up to size six were conducted. The analysis which follows concentrates on the five- and six-animal tests of dominance.

Method. Varley and Symmes measured pair-wise dominance outside the group context in two ways: (1) by determination of the number of peanuts procured by each animal in a series of seventy-five single nut feedings and (2) by examination of the frequency of initiation of aggressive interaction. (Compare Bernstein and Mason [1963] and Bernstein [1969] for similar measures of dominance.) In the event of discrepancies in ranks of food dominance and aggressive interaction, the authors assigned dominance on the basis of overall interaction. All pair-wise data were collected during the last month of observation.

In the analyses which follow, the pair-wise data are used to predict dominance relations among five animals in the colony and among animals in the full colony. Only one adjustment has been made to the actual pair-wise data. In order to illustrate the effectiveness of the method in instances of ties, the two cases in which food dominance rank and aggressive dominance rank conflict have been treated as ties.

In order to apply the model, the data for the six animals (represented by the symbols A through F in order of stable dominance rank in the full colony) are translated into graphs. Dominance in each paired relation is represented by a positive line directed from the dominant member to the subordinate member and a negative line directed from the subordinate member to the dominant member of the pair. Equality is represented by two positive lines joining the members of the pair (see Table 5.4).

After application of the procedure described above, it was determined that all points which were reachable by positive paths in the six-animal group were reachable in two steps. All points reachable by positive paths in the five-animal group were reachable in one step. The balance measures which result from application of equations (5.8) and (5.9) are presented in Tables 5.5 and 5.6.

Table 5.4
Matrices Representing Pair-Wise Relations among Members of One Six-Member and One Five-Member Group of Rhesus Macaques[a]

	A	B	C	D	E	F		B	C	D	E	F
A	0	1	1	1	1	1	B	0	-1	1	1	1
B	-1	0	-1	1	1	1	C	1	0	1	1	1
C	-1	1	0	1	1	1	D	1	-1	0	1	1
D	-1	1	-1	0	1	1	E	-1	-1	-1	0	-1
E	-1	-1	-1	-1	0	1	F	-1	-1	1	1	0
F	-1	-1	-1	1	1	0						

[a]Constructed from data reported in Varley and Symmes (1966). Data have been adjusted so that B=D and F=D. These pairs had conflicting ranks on the two primary measures of dominance reported by the investigators prior to introduction of a third measure to remove the ties. In each instance D was subordinate on the third measure.

Table 5.5
Local Balance Measures, Predicted Dominance Rank and Observed Dominance Rank among Five Rhesus Macaques

ANIMAL	MEASURE OF LOCAL BALANCE	PREDICTED RANK	OBSERVED RANK
B	.750	2.5	3
C	1.000	1	1
D	.750	2.5	4
E	.000	5	5
F	.500	4	2

$B(G) = .600$

$r_{op} = .675$

Table 5.6
Local Balance Measures, Predicted Dominance Rank and Observed Dominance Rank among Six Rhesus Macaques

ANIMAL	MEASURE OF LOCAL BALANCE	PREDICTED RANK	OBSERVED RANK
A	1.000	1	1
B	.600	3.5	2
C	.800	2	3
D	.600	3.5	4
E	.000	6	5
F	.455	5	6

$B(G) = .574$

$r_{op} = .843$

RESULTS

The data in Tables 5.5 and 5.6 indicate that the six-animal group has a structural balance measure of .574 while the five-animal group has a structural balance measure of .600. Hence, neither structure is balanced. If the group members in the full colony are ordered on the basis of their respective measures of local balance, the predicted ordering is as follows: $A > C > B = D > F > E$. The Spearman rank correlation coefficient of this predicted ordering to the actual ordering as recorded by trained observers is .843.

When the alpha animal is removed from the colony and group members are again ordered on the basis of their measures of local balance, the predicted ordering is: $C > B = D > F > E$. This predicted order is correlated to the actual order of rank determined in the five-animal group at .675.

These results suggest that the measure of local balance can be used to predict larger group relations from pair-wise data within a reasonable level of accuracy, even in cases in which ties in the data exist.

DISCUSSION

The results of the analysis of data taken from studies of dominance relations in animal groups have several implications. First, measures of structural balance appear to be useful for distinguishing groups which have hierarchical relations from groups which do not. It appears that groups which have measures of 1.00 are undifferentiated. That is, no member of the group can influence any other member of the group either directly or indirectly. On the other hand, groups which have balance measures less than 1.00 have some hierarchical elements.

Second, the measure of local balance appears to provide a means of predicting the character of a structure of dominance relations, which is created from the aggregation of several pairs of dominance relations. The rank order of animals based on the measure of local balance approximates the rank order based on observations of group behavior. The Spearman correlation coefficients of actual to predicted rank are reasonably high. It is important to note that the more information there is which exists on pairs, the higher correlation coefficients will be. For example, when total interaction data are used to break the ties in the Varley and Symmes data (as the investigators did) and measures of local balance are recalculated, the predicted and actual values for the five- and six-animal groups are correlated at .900 and .810, respectively. The theory of signed directed graphs is capable of utilizing information on multiple social relations and thus adding data on other relations, for example, grooming or sexual relations, might be expected to improve predictions generated by the model.

SUMMARY

While dominance relations have been observed and described in a variety of animal species, it has been generally difficult if not impossible to predict dominance orders in triads and larger groups from knowledge of pair-wise interaction. The problem appears to be exacerbated by the existence of ties and triangular relations. This chapter has pointed up the similarity of this problem to problems found in the study of power and influence relations in human groups. It has been suggested that pair-wise dominance relations may be aggregated in a manner similar to that proposed in a reformulation of a theory of social power. A model based on that reformulation has been applied to data from animal groups with a reasonable degree of success. It is suggested that the addition of information about a variety of social relationships rather than one or two will improve the accuracy of predictions from the model.

NOTES

1. Readers familiar with Emerson's work will recognize (5.1) as a statement of *net power*. Since (5.1) conforms closely to the definition of power proposed by Weber (and Emerson), this quantity will be called power. Thus, the confusion resulting from Emerson's use of D_{ba} as power is avoided. See Walker (1977) for discussion of this issue.

2. Emerson and his associates (see Stolte and Emerson, 1976; Cook and Emerson, 1978) have attempted to extend the theory to larger groups by using the conception of power network. Their success in those attempts rests on the ability to treat various group members as occupants of either of two social roles. The conception is realistically if not theoretically dyadic.

3. Although Figure 5.1a is the case in which A and B are not joined by a dependence relation, it is a special case of balance which is referred

to as vacuous balance (cf. Cartwright and Harary, 1956). As in Figure 5.1d, neither actor can influence the other.

4. A measure of structural balance equal to 0 can never be realized since that would require a group in which there are no relations of low dependence. By definition, a pair which is connected by a high dependence relation must also be connected by a low dependence relation. The converse of that statement is not true and structural balance measures of 1.00 are possible.

REFERENCES

Bachrach, P., and Baratz, M. *Power and Poverty*. Oxford University Press, New York, 1970.

Berge, C. *Graph Theory and Its Applications*. Wiley, New York, 1962.

Bernstein, I.S. Stability of the status hierarchy in a pigtail monkey group (*Macaca nemestrina*). *Anim. Behav.* 17:452-58, 1969.

Bernstein, I.S., and Mason, W.A. Group formation by rhesus monkeys. *Anim. Behav.* 11:28-31, 1963.

Bernstein, I.S., and Sharpe, L.G. Social roles in a rhesus monkey group. *Behaviour* 26:91-104, 1966.

Cartwright, D., and Harary, F. Structural balance: A generalization of Heider's theory. *Psychol. Rev.* 63:277-93, 1956.

Cook, K.S., and Emerson, R.M. Power, equity and commitment in exchange networks. *Am. Soc. Rev.* 43:721-39, 1978.

Dahl, R.A. The concept of power. *Behav. Sci.* 2:201-15, 1957.

Emerson, R.M. Power-dependence relations. *Am. Soc. Rev.* 27:31-41, 1962.

Emerson, R.M. Exchange theory, part I: A psychological basis for social exchange. In: *Sociological Theories in Progress*, vol. 2. J. Berger, M. Zelditch, Jr., and B. Anderson (Eds.), Houghton Mifflin, Boston, pp. 38-57, 1972a.

Emerson, R.M. Exchange theory, part II: Exchange relations, exchange networks and groups as exchange systems. In: *Sociological Theories in Progress*, vol. 2, J. Berger, M. Zelditch, Jr., and B. Anderson, (Eds.), Houghton Mifflin, Boston, pp. 58-87, 1972b.

Flament, C. *Applications of Graph Theory to Group Structure*. Prentice-Hall, Englewood Cliffs, NJ, 1963.

Harary, F. On the notion of balance of a signed digraph. *Mich. Math. J.* 2:143-46, 1953-54.

Harary, F.; Norman, R.Z.; and Cartwright, D. *Structural Models*. Wiley, New York, 1965.

Hinde, R.A. *Biological Bases of Human Social Behavior*. McGraw-Hill, New York, 1974.

Jolly, A. *The Evolution of Primate Behavior*. Macmillan, New York, 1972.

Landau, H.G. On dominance relations and the structure of animal societies: I. Effect of inherent characteristics. *Bull. Math. Biophys.* 13:1-19, 1951.

Maslow, A.H. The role of dominance in the social and sexual behavior of infrahuman primates: IV. The determination of hierarchy in pairs and in a group. *J. Genet. Psychol.* 49:161-98, 1936.

Mason, W.A. The effects of social restriction on the behavior of rhesus monkeys: III. Dominance tests. *J. Comp. Physiol. Psychol.* 54:694-99, 1961.

Murchison, C. The experimental measurement of a social hierarchy in *Gallus domesticus:* IV. Loss of body weight under conditions of mild starvation as a function of social dominance. *J. Gen. Psychol.* 12:296-312, 1935.

Schjelderup-Ebbe, T. Social behavior in birds. In: *A Handbook of Social Psychology*. C.A. Murchison (Ed.), Clark University Press, Worcester, MA., pp. 947-73, 1935.

Shapley, L., and Shubik, M. A method for evaluating the distribution of power in a committee system. *Am. Polit. Sci. Rev.* 48:787-92, 1954.

Stolte, J., and Emerson, R.M. Structural inequality: Position and power in network structures. In: *Behavior Theory In Sociology*. R. Hamblin and J. Kunkel (Eds.), Trans-Action, New York, pp. 131-49, 1976.

Taylor, H.F. *Balance in Small Groups*. Van Nostrand Reinhold, New York, 1970.

Varley, M., and Symmes, D. The hierarchy of dominance in a group of macaques. *Behaviour* 27:54-75, 1966.

Walker, H.A. Power and dependence relations revisited: An alternative conception. Unpublished manuscript, Department of Sociology, Stanford University, Stanford, CA, 1977.

Warren, J.M., and Maroney, R.J. Competitive social interaction between monkeys. *J. Soc. Psychol.* 48:223-33, 1958.

Weber, M. *The Theory of Social and Economic Organization*, Free Press, New York, 1947.

Wilson, E.O. *Sociobiology*. Belknap, Cambridge, MA, 1975.

6

The Regulatory Effect of Social Rank on Behavior after Amphetamine Administration

Suzanne N. Haber and Patricia R. Barchas

Of the variety of drugs which have been utilized in experiments with small social groups of primates (Machiyama et al., 1970; Redmond et al., 1971; McKinney et al., 1971; Crowley et al., 1974; Garver et al., 1975; Schiorring, 1977, 1979), amphetamine is especially interesting. Studies done both behaviorally and pharmacologically show that it has qualitatively similar physiological and psychological effects in animals and in humans. Although information regarding the interface between drug effects and social-environmental conditions is limited, it is known that the presence or absence of a social group interacts with behaviors that can be elicited by drug administration. Some behaviors appear only in social groups and are not seen in isolation, that is, drug-related aggressive behaviors, while the social group suppresses other drug-linked behaviors that are observed at higher dosages, that is, drug-induced stereotypy (Haber et al., 1981). While the importance of presence or absence of a social environment has been demonstrated (De Feudis, 1981), consideration has not been given to the social structure or individual relationships within the group. The role of social rank in regulating behavior when behavior has been artifically altered by amphetamine administration is explored in this chapter. Rhesus macaques are used as subjects. Hierarchical structures are characteristic of their social order and literature documents similar effects of amphetamine on humans and rhesus, suggesting that cautious extrapolation from the animal social model to the human condition may be reasonable. In contrast to assumptions often made that the drug effects are either completely constant across subjects or are totally individual, the study tests the hypothesis that the effects will be in part dependent upon the social position of the actor.

METHODS

The methods have been fully described elsewhere (Haber et al., 1981). Briefly, the study was carried out on two colonies of rhesus monkeys (*Macaca mulatta*). In each colony, relationships had been developed over a period of at least three months and were stable. The first colony consisted of four adult monkeys (two males and two females), and five adult animals composed the second colony (one male and four females until the colony had stabilized when, for reasons external to the study, the adult male was removed). They were housed and had free movement in a room 8 × 8 × 7 feet and 8 × 12 × 14 feet, respectively. All animals were fed ad lib and had a constant water supply. They were trained to come out of the enclosure each morning and were placed in individual cages where they received fruit and a sugar cube which contained either amphetamine or water. All animals began by receiving 0.1 mg/kg of amphetamine. During the first five days of administration, the dose was increased 0.1 mg/kg in daily increments. Since it was imperative that the animals be able to interact with one another during the last two weeks, dose adjustments were made, depending on each animal's ability to tolerate the amphetamine without crossing the threshold upon which stereotypic behavior began to emerge. Table 6.1 shows the final amphetamine dose for each animal.

Baseline data, with all animals receiving sugar cubes with water, were collected for three weeks. At this point, one animal chosen

Table 6.1
Final Amphetamine Dose for Each Animal

Subject	Weight (kg)	Last Dose/Weight
Colony I		
Fr	6.85	1.5
Pe	5	1.1
Ga	8.6	1.9
B	5	2.1
Colony II		
Gi	5.5	1.8
Se	5	2.0
Be	3.3	2.4
Bt	5.9	1.7

randomly from the group received amphetamine once a day for three weeks, while all other animals received water. Before any other member of the group was given amphetamine, all animals received water for an additional three weeks following the drug trial; therefore new baselines were collected before the drug trial of each animal. A final three-week baseline was collected at the end of the drug trials.

Behavioral observations were taken four days a week, both in the morning, one hour after drug or water administration, and in the afternoon, five to seven hours after administration. Data were collected on each animal for thirty minutes, yielding a total 150 minutes of daily behavioral observation.

To estimate duration of events, point-in-time sampling at every thirty seconds was used with such behaviors as "groom" and "sit tense." Interrater reliability remained high (85 percent) in each behavioral category throughout the entire study. For all social interactions, the animals involved were noted, as well as who was responsible for initiating the interaction.

Changes in measures between drug and baseline periods were assessed by the Friedman two-way analysis of variance test (two-tailed, degrees of freedom 5). Correlations between measures were assessed by the Spearman rank correlation coefficient (one-tailed). All tests and tables of significance were nonparametric and derived from Siegel (1956).

RESULTS

The first section gives the results for relevant behaviors across all animals without regard to position in the group. The second analyzes these with respect to animals' position in the hierarchy of the group in order to examine the role rank plays in mediating behavioral changes elicited by the administration of amphetamine. Analysis of affiliative and agonistic behaviors not only across all animals but also with regard to rank will clarify whether social modification of the effects of amphetamine on primate behavior is through social parameters such as position in the hierarchical structure, as well as by membership in a social group (Haber, 1981). (Analyses relevant to an animal model of paranoia have been described in Haber et al. [1981].)

Results across Animals without Regard to "Rank"

The route of delivery of amphetamine was effective as evidenced by the decrease in time spent eating and sleeping for all animals (significance $p < .01$). Changes in behavior did not result merely from simple increases or decreases in ongoing behaviors since the changes were not correlated with baseline activity. For example, as can be seen in Figure 6.1, animals who oriented frequently during the averaged baseline periods did not necessarily exhibit the highest increase in orienting response due to the drug. This was also true when the drug period was compared to the baseline immediately preceding the drug period.

Agonistic Behavior. Overall agonistic behavior increased for each animal during its drug period ($p < .01$) (combined submissive and threatening behaviors). However, overall agonistic behavior

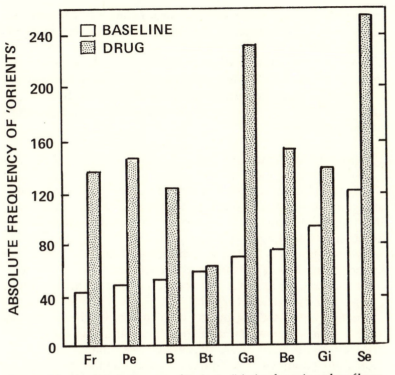

Figure 6.1 Absolute frequency of "orients." Animals are in order of base-line activity (lowest to highest). Based on absolute frequency of orients for both baseline averages and drug period.

of the group during drug periods did not increase. That is, animals not receiving amphetamine did not increase their agonistic behavior during periods when other animals were receiving drugs nor was there an increase in agonistic behavior towards the target animal. Thus, increases in agonistic behavior were due to the target animals' response to the drug and did not reflect general disruption in the group due to amphetamine administration nor to provocation from other members of the colony.

Both categories "sit tense" and "orient" were correlated with increases in agonistic behaviors ($rs = .71$, $p < .05$ and $rs = .88$, $p < .01$, respectively), so that animals with a high proportional increase in "sit tense" and "orient" categories were also the animals with the high increases in agonistic behaviors. Thus, a cluster of hypervigilant-threat behaviors following a similar trend emerged during the drug periods.

Proximity Measures and Affiliative Behaviors. No changes in proximity or affiliative behaviors were revealed in the across animals analysis. While some target animals increased the number of grooming bouts with other animals, others decreased in number or did not change.

Results with Regard to Rank

Behavioral interactions were considered by rank in the hierarchy. In these analyses, outcome of agonistic interactions during the baseline period was used to order the animals according to dominance (rank) in the groups.

Agonistic Behaviors. Not all animals increased agonistic behavior in the same way. When submissive and threatening behaviors were analyzed separately, there was no significant effect in either category by itself. However, when submissive behaviors by subordinate animals were grouped with threats by the dominant animals, there was a dramatic and significant drug effect ($p <$ .01) (see Figure 6.2). Thus, submissive test animals submitted more, while dominant test animals threatened more during their drug periods (Figure 6.3). Animals who were most submissive in the group displayed more submissive behaviors during drug periods, such as fear grimaces, crouching and turning away, as well as more avoidance behavior. Dominant animals threatened, chased and attacked other members of the group more often during their drug period than during baseline periods.

As mentioned, these changes were due to the target animals' response to the drug since there were no increases of agonistic behaviors directed toward the target animal (Figure 6.3). Submissive target animals were not threatened more even though they increased in their submissive behaviors. Likewise, dominant target animals were not submitted to more although their threatening behaviors increased during their drug period.

The direction of agonistic behavior was not random. Dominant animals threatened downward in the hierarchy and subordinate

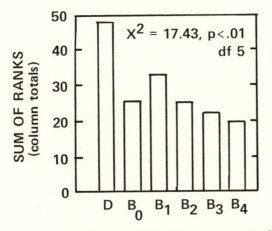

Figure 6.2 Sum of ranks: Submits by subordinate target animals grouped with threats by dominant target animals. D = drug period for each animal; B_o = baseline following each drug period for each animal; B_1 = baseline 1; B_2 = baseline 2; B_3 = baseline 3; B_4 = baseline 4.

animals submitted upward. Middle-rank animals showed an increase in both behaviors. Moreover, submits and threats not only were in the proper direction, but were directed toward the animals with whom the target animal had the greatest competition for rank. However, animals increased their respective agonistic behaviors without appropriate cues or responses from other animals. At these doses amphetamine alters individual specific behaviors in a way not necessarily predictable from nondrug behavior, while those behaviors associated with rank in the social hierarchy are altered in a way consistent with the animal's nondrug position in the hierarchy.

Other Behaviors Affected by Rank. While a cluster of hypervigilant-threat behaviors emerged across animals during drug periods (see Figure 6.4), it was of great interest to note that the lowest rank animal in each group had the lowest proportional increase in each catagory ($p < .01$). That is, if the rank order of proportional change is given for each hypervigilant behavior in each group, the low-ranking animal had the lowest proportional increase in

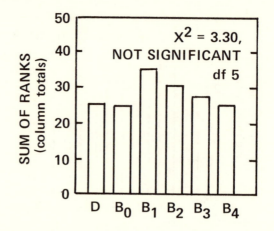

Figure 6.3 Sum of ranks: Threats directed toward subordinate target animals grouped with submits directed toward dominant target animals. D = drug period for each animal; B_o = baseline following each drug period for each animal; B_1 = baseline 1; B_2 = baseline 2; B_3 = baseline 3; B_4 = baseline 4.

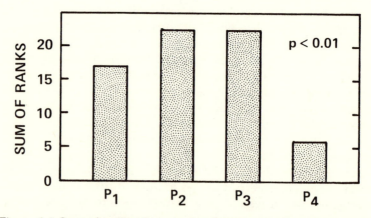

Figure 6.4 Sum of ranks of proportional increase in the cluster of hypervigilant-threat behaviors: Percentage increase in sit tense, orient and agonistic behaviors. P_1 = position 1 in the hierarchy; P_2 = position 2 in the hierarchy; P_3 = position 3 in the hierarchy; P_4 = position 4 in the hierarchy.

every case (agonistic, sit tense, orient). This was not due to the correlation between measures, since for each of the other six animals no such relationship existed.

There were no changes in the number of overall grooming bouts or time spent grooming. However, those low in the hierarchy either did not change the number of grooming bouts or decreased them, while all high ranking animals that were normally groomed by other animals each spent more time being groomed during their own drug period.

Case Example: An Animal Changes Rank

B was the only animal who was in both colonies. When B was a member of Colony I she was a frightened and isolated animal. Frequently she would sit in the corner, roll up in a ball and pull her hair out, a behavior that dramatically increased with amphetamine administration. The lowest-ranked animal in Colony I, B rarely groomed or was groomed by other animals. She actively avoided others in the group, and during her drug period she did not socialize at all with members of the group. Her submissive behavior dramatically increased during her drug period, and the cluster of hypervigilant behaviors showed the lowest proportional increase of the group on every measure (Figure 6.5).

When placed into Colony II, her adjustment in the new social setting was remarkable, primarily due to the dominant male's favor. No longer an isolated animal, she participated in grooming and interacted with all members of the group. She became a social animal and was the dominant female (Figure 6.6). Since it was almost one year since she had been in Colony I, and her behavior had changed, she was evaluated as a different subject (Be).

During her drug period while a member of this group, she did not dramatically increase her submissive behaviors as she had done previously, but, as the dominant female in the group, she did dramatically increase threatening behavior. The time spent being groomed by other animals also increased during Be's drug period. It is also interesting to note that during this period her rank in proportional changes in hypervigilant drug related behaviors was no longer significantly low (Figure 6.7). Her drug-related, idiosyncratic, "individual-specific" behaviors were the same although decreased from that observed in Colony I.

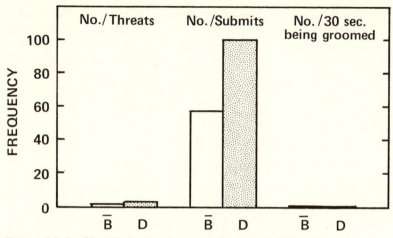

Figure 6.5 Profile of behavior during drug period of *B/Be* when she was
lowest ranking member of Colony I.

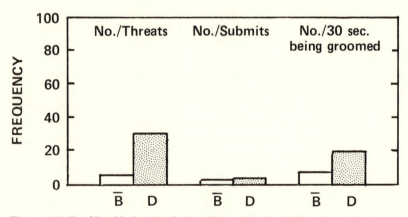

Figure 6.6 Profile of behavior during drug period of *B/Be* when she was
a relatively high ranking member of Colony II.

DISCUSSION

Understanding the hierarchical relations in the group clarifies
the effects of amphetamine on agonistic behavior. Animals increased these behaviors selectively according to rank. Thus, high-
ranking animals threatened more while low-ranking animals sub-

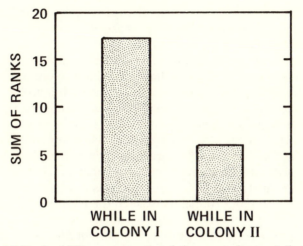

Figure 6.7 Rank of *B/Be* on proportional changes in hypervigilant drug-related behaviors in Colony I and in Colony II.

mitted more. While the increases in time spent during grooming for high-ranking animals was not significant due to the small sample size, the trend was seen in all high-ranking animals. Three of these animals actively solicited to be groomed while in their drug period, and the grooming resulted in a dramatic decrease in the hypervigilant behaviors, sitting tense and orienting. It therefore seemed to be an anxiety-reducing scheme. Such mechanisms have been reported to exist in primates (Mason, 1960; Lindburg, 1973). Of course, low-ranking rhesus may not have the option for such solicitation, which would also account for the difference by rank observed in grooming behavior.

The low proportional increases in the hypervigilant cluster of behaviors seen with low ranking animals were not due to a ceiling effect determined by number of thirty-second observations available, since the increases represent only a fraction of the time allowed. It is possible that each animal has an unknown individual limit of the amount of behavior he can exhibit during a particular timeframe. Equally possible, however, is the notion that low-ranking animals have learned that in the face of disturbance their ability to positively control the environment through their behavior is limited, while high-ranking animals can exert more control. Therefore, during their disruptive drug period, high-ranking animals exhibit a greater increase in agonistic behaviors, orienting and sitting tense.

The argument that rank can affect drug response is illustrated by the case of the only animal that was in both colonies, *B/Be*. In one colony *B* was the lowest-ranked animal, while in the other colony, she was the highest-ranked animal. During her drug period in Colony I she dramatically increased submissive behaviors, was not groomed by other animals, and had a low proportional increase in the hypervigilant-threat behaviors. In Colony II, she did not show an increase in submissive behaviors, but rather an increase of threatening behaviors; she was groomed more, and she had a high proportional increase in the hypervigilant-threat behaviors. Her response to amphetamine was consistent with her rank in the respective groups. The case of *B/Be* is illustrative of the data analyzed statistically: amphetamine altered her interactive behaviors in a manner consistent with the rank she held in each colony.

Animals increased their respective agonistic behavior in the absence of appropriate cues or responses from other animals. While behaviors were appropriately directed, they occurred at inappropriate times, and therefore appeared to be out of the context of the normal social situation. Rank determinants of observed agonistic interactions illustrates how, at the dose used, amphetamine affects the animal's behaviors, making them consistent with its normal patterns although inappropriate to the immediate cues from the environment. The drug seems to have obscured the fine tuning made possible by cues from members of the immediate group.

Clearly, in the rhesus, an animal's position in the hierarchical structure of the group can have a profound effect on the response to amphetamine. However, the rhesus is well known to be a species in which social hierarchy is a major factor in group life and in the interindividual relationships which form. For other species, the effect of rank per se might be less dramatic as a social modulator of drug effects, but any organizational principles which importantly govern group relations could be used in a similar analysis. Remembering that the action of amphetamine is through alteration of the attentional centers of the brain, it is likely that behavioral reponses due to a variety of drugs, lesions, and social manipulations which are involved in attention are profoundly affected by the typical structure of the group, which for rhesus is the hierarchy.

Other psychoactive drugs also change behavior through direct and known actions on the central nervous system in the absence of altered environmental or sensory input. It should be possible to use such knowledge to develop research strategies in which selected drugs at varying doses are administered to social animals whose species clearly exhibits particular patterns of organization to assess the level of mental organization at which social structures such as hierarchies exert their regulatory effects on behavior.

REFERENCES

Crowley, T.J.; Stynes, A.J.; Hydinger, M.; and Kaufman, C. Ethanol, methamphetamine, pentobarbital, morphine, and monkey social behavior. *Arch. Gen. Psychiatry* 31:829-38, 1974.

De Feudis, F.V. Effects of social environment on cerebral morphology,chemistry and pharmacology. In: *Toward an Ecology of Brain.* R. Walsh (Ed.), SP Medical and Scientific Books, New York, pp. 71-98, 1981.

Garver, D.; Schlommer, F.; Maas, J.; and Davis, J. A schizophreniform behavioral psychosis mediated by dopamine. *Am. J. Psychiatry* 132:1, 1975.

Haber, S. Social factors in evaluating the effects of biological manipulation on aggressive behavior in nonhuman primates. In: *Biobehavioral Aspects of Aggression.* D. Hamburg and M. Trudeau (Eds.), Alan R. Liss, New York, pp. 41-49, 1981.

Haber, S.; Barchas, P.; and Barchas, J. A primate analog of amphetamine-induced behaviors in humans. *Biol. Psych.* 16:181-96, 1981.

Lindburg, D.G. Grooming behavior as a regulator of social interactions in rhesus monkeys. In: *Behavioral Regulators of Behavior in Primates.* C.R. Carpenter (Ed.), Associated University Press, New York, 1973.

Machiyama, Y.; Utena, H.; and Kikuchi, M. Behavioral disorders in Japanese monkeys produced by long-term administration of methamphetamine. *Proc. Jap. Acad.* 46:738, 1970.

McKinney, W.T.; Eising, R.G.; Morgan, E.C.; Suomi, J.J.; and Herlow,

H.F. Effects of reserpine on the social behavior of rhesus monkeys. *Dis. Ner. Sys. 32*:735-41, 1971.

Mason, W.A. Socially mediated reduction in emotional responses of young rhesus monkeys. *J. Abn. Soc. Psychol. 60*:100-04, 1960.

Redmond, D.E.; Maas, J.; Kling, A.; and Dekirminjian, H. Changes in primate social behavior after treatment with alpha-methyl-para-tyrosine. *Psychosom. Med. 33*:97-113, 1971.

Schiorring, E. Changes in individual and social behavior induced by amphetamine and related compounds in monkeys and man. In: *Cocaine and Other Stimulants*. E. Ellinwood and M. Kilbey (Eds.), Plenum Press, New York, pp. 481-522, 1977.

Schiorring, E. Social isolation and other behavioral changes in groups of adult vervet monkeys (*Ceropithecus aethiops*) produced by low, nonchronic doses of *d* amphetamine. *Psychopharmacology 64*:297-302, 1979.

Siegel, S. *Non-parametric Statistics for the Behavioral Sciences*. McGraw-Hill Book Co., New York, 1956.

7

An Attention-Regulating Function of Social Hierarchies: High Status, Attention, and the CNV Brain Wave

Patricia R. Barchas, William S. Jose II, Barbara A. Payne, and William A. Harris

Social hierarchies are a frequently recurring form of social relationships in groups which include two or more people. In small groups status hierarchies typically do not arise from either logical or conscious processes. They simply crystallize around any characteristic—state or trait, achieved or ascribed, imagined or real—which differentiates people. Even so, after one session of interaction under experimental conditions, participants can rank each other on who had the best ideas, gave the most guidance and had the most leadership ability with reasonably high agreement between them (Fisek, 1968). Behaviorally, higher-status group members are less likely to defer to or be influenced by lower-status group members (Whittaker, 1965) and are more likely to interrupt lower-status group members (Zimmerman and West, 1975), to perform more frequently (Curtis et al., 1975; Lockheed-Katz and Hall, 1976; Strodtbeck and Mann, 1956), to perform more rapidly (Connor, 1977), to be asked for information more often (Eskilson and Riley, 1976), and to be evaluated more positively by group members when quality of performance is held constant (Goldberg, 1958).

In prototypical form, behavioral differentiations cluster around group members (Bales, 1950, 1953; Bales and Slater, 1955; Heinicke and Bales, 1953) to produce a single, relatively stable "power and prestige" hierarchical order (Berger, 1958; Fisek and Ofshe, 1970) along which group members are arrayed independently of objectively measured task performance (Harvey, 1953; Sherif et al., 1955; Whyte, 1943). The regularity with which the relationship between position in the hierarchical structure and particular behavior appears is consistent with the view that relative location in the intangible hierarchy tells group members with whom and how they should interact, especially with regard to task-related behaviors. The phenomenon is clearly established. The research question at issue is how it happens.

We submit that recurrent forms of relationships embodied in hierarchical social structures are readily available frames of reference which provide aggregated individuals initial and pre-coordinated orientations to the social environment. The prepatterned orientations guide the actors as they determine what is relevant in particular social situations, which elements should be filtered out before conscious perception and to which they should pay attention and respond. As the preconsciously anticipated pattern of relations and their associated roles are realized in behavior, the group emerges. Behavior then reinforces the preconceived patterns of relationship. Under some circumstances, actors may jostle for position, but the structure itself is rarely in question. According to this formulation, social structures exert their influence chiefly through attentional processes which may occur out of the range of conscious awareness: Behavior is conditioned by attentional processes.

The notion that a positive association exists between position in a group's hierarchy and the way group members distribute attention is supported in the sociological literature, especially in terms of the high end of the continuum. Hollander's (1964) observation that higher-status persons are more attentive to the focal activities of the group is consistent with earlier statements made by Homans (1950) and Whyte (1943). A particular instance of our general conception of the relationship between comparative position in the hierarchy and attentional distribution, then, would be a predicted positive association between high status and heightened attention to task: Persons performing a task in a high status state should exhibit greater attention to task than when they perform the same task not in a high status state.

In order to operationalize this hypothesis, there is needed both a behavioral situation in which positional or status changes can be induced and a reliable index of prebehavioral attentional changes. Developments in both in the neurological (Kandel and Schwartz, 1981; Klatzky, 1975; Shagass, 1972) and the social sciences (Berger et al., 1980) made it possible to conduct a limited initial empirical study.

A brain wave pattern, the CNV (contingent negative variation), is sensitive to subtle changes in attention (Walter, 1964; Shagass, 1972; Callaway, 1975). Augmented under conditions of increased attention, the CNV is diminished under conditions of decreased attention. In experimental situations, the CNV occurs during the interval between occurrence of a warning signal indicating testing is about to begin and the signal that a motor response is required, as shown in Figure 7.1. An interval of one or two seconds is long enough for the CNV to develop fully (Callaway, 1975). As the CNV is locked to the eliciting stimuli, repeated trials are needed to permit background noise to be averaged out.

Although interindividual variation is high, within-individual constancy under the same conditions has been shown to exist with short test-retest intervals (one to three hours) and with longer test-retest intervals (two to eight days) (Roth et al., 1975; Shagass and Schwartz, 1961). Test-retest correlations of measurements within the same test situation are reported to range between .87 and .97 (Kooi and Bagchi, 1964). Therefore, this physiological measure may be used appropriately in experimental designs of the before-after type in which the treatment alters the attentional state of the subjects.

A two-phase experimental paradigm developed to study hierarchical processes (Berger et al., 1977) incorporates repeated trials and a before-after design in which the subject's status is altered by procedures which manipulate the subject's feeling of competence relative to another. Straightforwardly adaptable to requirements for studies in which attention-linked CNV brain-

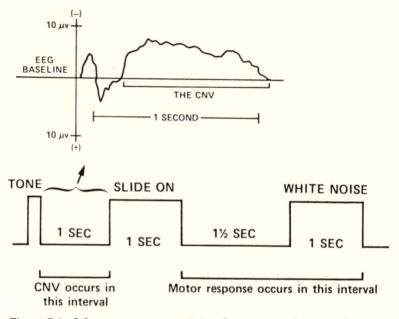

Figure 7.1. Schematic representation of sequence of events for each problem trial, with diagram of typical CNV wave.

waves are measured, the basic before-after, repeated trials design permits subjects to be used as their own controls; allows the nonrelevant, nonstimulus-linked activity to be averaged out; and has a standard postsession interview protocol with which to determine whether the subject actually met experimental criteria and was responsive to the manipulation. Paradigm-appropriate tasks have been developed and are available. Finally, there is a theoretical apparatus (Berger et al., 1977) which could be useful in future work.

Because of the posited attention-regulating role of position in a social structure, the operational hypothesis is that subjects will have a significantly higher CNV concomitant with task performance after the competence manipulation into a high status state compared with when they performed the task before the manipulation while not in a high status state.

PROCEDURES

Each of the ten male college student subjects was first seated in a briefing room along with a confederate whom he could not see because of a screen divider between them. After a general description of the experimental procedures, the subject was asked to sign a presession consent form. The subject was told that the study would be in two parts. He was instructed that in the first part each person would work separately in each of two phases as electroencephalographic (EEG) recordings were made; and that in the second part of the study, he and his "partner" (actually a confederate) were to work together as a team on problems similar to those in the first part of the study. Only the first part of the study was actually run. It was explained that the first part consisted of two series of problems called Relational Insight, and that after the first series, scores would be reported to both the subject and his "partner" and related to the "national standards" for this test. The Relational Insight test consists of a series of "Asian" characters said to be from a primitive language no longer used. In reality, Relational Insight is a fictitious ability which is sufficiently believable to produce the status manipulation. The subject was to decide for each problem whether the symbol expressed a concrete or abstract meaning in the language. He recorded his answer by pressing the appropriate button on the arm of his chair. After the first set of problems, the subject was told that he scored thirty-seven correct out of forty, placing him in the "above average" category on the "national standards" for this test; and that his "partner" scored nine correct out of forty, placing him in the "poor" category. The subject was then given another set of Relational Insight problems to work on. At completion, the subject was interviewed to determine the effectiveness of the manipulation, debriefed, paid, asked to sign a postsession consent form, and released.

Each problem was presented tachistoscopically from a slide. While the subject was working on the two-slide series, electrical activity of the brain was recorded on FM tape. The electroencephalogram (EEG) was recorded from the vertex (C_z) referenced to the linked ear lobes. A mid-forehead lead grounded the subject. The electrooculogram (EDG) was recorded on the infra-orbital and supra-orbital ridges directly above and below the right pupil. A pin electrode was used at the vertex, and Grass gold cup disc electrodes elsewhere.

For each problem presentation, the subject first heard a tone (800 H_z for 100 msec. at 75db SPL, presented binaurally through headphones) which indicated that the slide was about to appear. One second after the tone, the slide was shown for one second. If the subject had not made a decision one and one-half seconds after the slide went off, he heard a white noise to remind him to respond immediately.

Analog signals for both the EEG and the EOG in this time-locked interval were recorded for each trial on magnetic tape. Cumulative waveforms were generated for each slide series using a Fabritek signal averaging computer. The averaged signals were then graphed on an X-Y plotter and converted to digital form.

The Corby and Kopell (1972) procedure for removing eye movement artifact from the EEG record was followed. The subject-specific percentage of the EOG was subtracted from the EEG after signal averaging, yielding the data used in the analysis.

Subjects were sorted according to the effectiveness of the status manipulation, as revealed by the postsession interview. A subject was considered to have formed a higher evaluation of self than other with regard to competency on the task and therefore to have been manipulated into a higher status state only if he gave evidence that he met all of the following criteria: (1) he believed there was another person going through the study with him and that he would be working with that person in a later phase of the study; (2) he believed there were right and wrong answers to the test; (3) he believed that the scores reported for both himself and his partner were true; and (4) he remembered his score on the test relative to his partner's score. If the subject gave positive evidence that he met all of the above criteria, he was classified as having been effectively and strongly manipulated into a high status expectation state: five subjects met these criteria. The remaining five subjects failed to meet one or more of the above criteria and were not so classified. They were considered to have been ineffectively manipulated.

ANALYSIS

Tables 7.1 and 7.2 array the before-and-after-manipulation CNV amplitude scores for both sets of subjects as well as the difference scores. Visual inspection of the difference column shows that for those subjects classified as having met experimental criteria, five of five subjects increased CNV amplitude after the status manipulation, as hypothesized.

Table 7.1 presents the CNV amplitude measures for those subjects who met experimental criteria. In all five cases, the absolute value of the amplitude increased in the second slide series, after subjects assumed the higher status state. A one-tailed t-test for paired samples was statistically significant ($D = 3.26$, $S_D = 0.62$, $t = 11.76$, $df = 4$, $p < .0005$). The increased amplitude on the second slide set is consistent with the hypothesis of increased attention to task.

As is seen in Table 7.2, four of the five subjects who did not

Table 7.1
CNV Amplitude Measures before and after Manipulation for Those Subjects Who Met Experimental Criteria

Subject	Before Manipulation Max. Amplitude (μv)	After Manipulation Max. Amplitude (μv)	Difference (Before - After)
A	-7.00	-10.50	+3.50
B	+1.20	-1.47	+2.67
C	-6.12	-8.83	+2.71
D	-5.62	-8.87	+3.25
E	-4.94	-9.11	+4.17
Mean	-4.50	-7.76	

Paired $\underline{t}$ statistic for before/after difference of means test:

$\underline{t} = 11.76$, $\underline{df} = 4$, $\underline{p} < 0.0005$.

Table 7.2
CNV Amplitude Measures before and after Manipulation for Those Subjects Who Did Not Meet Experimental Criteria

Subject	Before Manipulation Max. Amplitude (μv)	After Manipulation 2d Slide Series Max. Amplitude (μv)	Difference (Before - After)
F	-9.18	-6.38	-2.80
G	-3.00	-15.25	+12.25
H	-16.41	-9.05	-7.36
I	-6.66	-5.64	-1.02
J	-10.17	-5.71	-4.26
Mean	-9.08	-8.41	

Paired t statistic for before/after difference of means test:

t = .20, df = 4, p > 0.10.

meet experimental criteria showed a decreased amplitude on the second slide set after manipulation. No statistically significant differences between phases were found for those subjects not effectively manipulated ($D = 0.67$, $S_D = 7.59$, $df = 4$, $t = .20$, $p > 0.10$). The groups' decreased amplitude on the second slide set is consistent with reduced attention to task, as fatigue and habituation would lead one to expect in the absence of a countervailing force (Shagass, 1972).

INTERPRETATION

The effectively manipulated subjects responded as hypothesized. The increase of CNV is consistent with the hypothesized relationship between differentiated and high status and the CNV. While direction of change is the important consideration, it should be noted that individually the ineffectively manipulated subjects exhibit the greatest magnitude of change. On reflection, this may be explained by the fact that the hierarchical, status-linked changes are normative. It is therefore reasonable that physiological as well as behavioral variability between persons who are alike with respect to the hierarchical structure should be similarly constrained by it.

The data on the CNV measures yield to more than one interpretation. It does seem to be the case, as we have argued, that the high status-through-competence manipulation, when strong and effective, counteracts fatigue and habituation to task and increases the magnitude of the CNV. This interpretation is supported by the finding of increased CNV amplitude for the subjects who were effectively manipulated combined with the finding of no significant increase for those who were ineffectively manipulated, with four of the five decreasing.

The ineffectively manipulated subjects are representative of subjects whose behavior is ordinarily eliminated from analysis in typical social psychological experiments due to violation of scope conditions. While it is only on the effectively manipulated subjects that the hypotheses may be tested, for this exploratory study into how a social and a physiological system might interact through attentional processes, those who were not manipulated are an interesting comparison group because they had been through the same physical and manipulation procedures as the target group.

For subjects who were classified as having not met experimental criteria, four of the five show decreased CNV amplitude scores. The fifth subject of the group, G, is an anomaly. He had the greatest increase of any subject in the study. On the postsession interview schedule, he was recorded as having remembered his and his partner's scores and as having thought there were right and wrong answers, thereby achieving two of the four criteria for meeting experimental scope conditions. However, he "wondered about the partner because they were separated" and was skeptical about the accuracy of the scores "because he was highest," thereby casting doubt on whether he thought the scores reported for himself and his partner were true. Subject G was appropriately classified as having not met experimental criteria according to the rules established before the study began.

Other information recorded about G indicates that while he was "skeptical," he also was "proud of never getting a hiss to tell him to respond faster" and was working to please the experimenter, an attractive young graduate student. While G may not have been manipulated into a high status, he nevertheless seems to have been quite engaged and attentive to the situation for other reasons.

The mean CNV amplitude before manipulation for the effectively manipulated subjects is -4.50, while it is -9.08 for the ineffectively manipulated subjects as a group. If subject G were eliminated for reasons described above, the difference would be even larger. The difference in group means suggests that subjects who do not respond to this and similar manipulations, and are therefore usually eliminated from analysis in behavioral social psychological studies for not meeting the conditions of the experiment, may be in an initially physiologically or psychologically different state than are the "good" subjects. Alternatively, the ineffectively manipulated subjects also may have performed the first set of problems so attentively that further increase was not feasible or, for some subjects, the high status manipulation may have induced disengagement once the subject achieved "success" in the situation. Such conjectures are consistent with values from the ineffectively manipulated group in which subjects F, H and J have the highest before-manipulation scores of all subjects.

Thus, it is not clear whether the ineffectively manipulated subjects failed to show regular increases in CNV amplitude because of the weakness of the manipulation, or whether they represent one or more subgroups who, for reasons of physiological or psychological individual differences, are either resistant to such manipulations or react differently to them. It seems reasonable to suggest that there may be an interaction effect between amplitude of the CNV and susceptibility to the effects of social status changes such as the one manipulated in this study. The further studies necessary for clarification should minimally include a no-manipulation condition and increased Ns in all cells.

The discussion about the ineffectively manipulated subjects should not obscure the focal point: The high competence manipulation did have the effect of increasing the amplitude of the CNV for those subjects classified as strongly manipulated. Whether the data are taken to suggest distinct subgroups or not, there is evidence of a positive relationship between CNV amplitude and manipulation into a high competence state relative to another individual, as hypothesized from the high-status, heightened-attention, increased-CNV argument.

DISCUSSION

This essay has shown the feasibility of combining a form of hierarchical relationship which can be reliably induced in the laboratory with a physiological measure of attention in order to begin to explore posited attention-regulating functions of social structures. It suggests that social hierarchies may function as internally represented schemas for social interaction which modify behavior at a preconscious level by regulating attention. In capsule, it has argued that the orientation to the environment provided by first knowledge of and then position in the hierarchy of informal task groups gives group members a general strategy for coordinated behavior. The strategy is executed, at least in part, by differentially directed attentional focus and intensity. The resulting group structure presumably acquires content and meaning according to the situation, with specific interactional content and style being further specified by other features of the group, by individual differences and by the larger social context.

Thus, in any given situation, the behavioral regularities associated with hierarchical position and social status are the result of physiological and social processes which function independently of particular individuals or particular characteristics. As the group-level process differentially engages and coordinates the attentional and response mechanisms of individuals, mapping them into the hierarchical structure, the hierarchy acts as a prefabricated frame of reference which provides group members with a differentiated but shared orientation to the social environment. As group members continue to pay attention and respond to those elements of the situation which each judges to be most relevant according to his own location in the hierarchy, situation-specific features of interpersonal interaction are specified which assure that the distribution of rights, privileges and responsibilities tends to be maintained. This has the signal consequence that group members' behavior is mutually coordinated and complementary over time.

ACKNOWLEDGMENTS

The authors would like to thank Drs. B.S. Kopell and W.T. Roth for their help; to acknowledge support from the Harry Frank Guggenheim Foundation and the Office of Naval Research; to thank Sue Poage for her able secretarial assistance; and to acknowledge the intellectual support of the Stanford Department of Sociology.

REFERENCES

Bales, R.F. *Interaction Process Analysis.* Addison-Wesley, Reading, MA, 1950.

Bales, R.F. The equilibrium problem in small groups. In: *Working Papers in the Theory of Action.* T. Parsons, R.F. Bales and E.H. Shils (Eds.), Free Press, Glencoe, IL, pp. 111-61, 1953.

Bales, R.F., and Slater, P. Role differentiation in small decision making groups. In: *Family, Socialization and Interaction Process.* T. Parsons and R.F. Bales (Eds.), Free Press, Glencoe, IL, pp. 259-306, 1955.

Berger, J. Relations between Performance, Rewards, and Action-Opportunities in Small Groups. Ph.D. dissertation, Harvard University, 1958.

Berger, J.; Fisek, M.H.; Norman, R.A.; and Zelditch, M., Jr. *Status Characteristics and Social Interaction: An Expectation States Approach.* Elsevier Scientific Publishing Co., New York, 1977.

Berger, J.; Rosenholtz, S.J.; and Zelditch, M., Jr. Status organizing processes. *Ann. Rev. Soc.,* vol. 6. Annual Reviews, Inc., Palo Alto, CA, pp. 479-508, 1980.

Callaway, E. *Brain Electrical Potentials and Individual Psychological Differences.* Grune and Stratton, New York, 1975.

Connor, T.L. Performance expectations and the initiation of problem solving attempts. *J. Math. Soc.* 5:187-98, 1977.

Corby, J., and Kopell, B.S. Differential contribution of blinks and vertical eye movements as artifacts in EEG recording. *Psychophysiology* 9:640-44, 1972.

Curtis, R.C.; Zanna, M.P.; and Campbell, W.W., Jr. Sex, fear of success and perceptions and performance of law school students. *Am. Educ. Res. J. 12*:287-97, 1975.

Eskilson, A., and Riley, M.G. Sex composition and leadership in small groups. *Sociometry 39*:183-94, 1976.

Fisek, M.H. The evolution of status structures and interaction in task oriented discussion groups. Ph.D. dissertation, Stanford University, 1968.

Fisek, M.H., and Ofshe, R. The process of status evolution. *Sociometry 33*:327-46, 1970.

Goldberg, P. Are women prejudiced against women? *Transaction 5*:28-30, 1958.

Harvey, O.J. An experimental approach to the study of status relations in informal groups. *Am. Soc. Rev. 18*:357-67, 1953.

Heinicke, C., and Bales, R.F. Developmental trends in the structure of small groups. *Sociometry 16*:7-38, 1953.

Hollander, E.P. *Leaders, Groups, and Influence.* Oxford, New York, 1964.

Homans, G.C. *The Human Group.* Harcourt, Brace and World, New York, 1950.

Kandel, E.R., and Schwartz, J.H. *Principles of Neural Science.* Elsevier, North Holland, New York, 1981.

Klatzky, R.L. *Human Memory: Structures and Processes.* W.H. Freeman and Co., San Francisco, 1975.

Kooi, K.A., and Bagchi, B.K. Visual evoked potentials in man: Normative data. *Ann. N.Y. Acad. Sci. 112*:254-69, 1964.

Lockheed-Katz, M.S., and Hall, K. Conceptualizing sex as a status characteristic: Application to leadership training strategies. *J. Soc. Iss. 32*:111-24, 1976.

Roth, W.T.; Kopell, B.S.; Tinklenberg, J.R.; Huntsberger, G.E.; and Kraemer, H.C. Reliability of contingent negative variation and the auditory evoked potential. *Electroencephalogr. Clin. Neurophysiol. 38*:45-50, 1975.

Shagass, C. *Evoked Brain Potentials in Psychiatry.* Plenum Press, New York, 1972.

Shagass, C., and Schwartz, M. Evoked aortical potentials and sensation in man. *J. Neuropsychiatry 2*:262-70, 1961.

Sherif, M.; White, B.J.; and Harvey, O.J. Status in experimentally produced groups. *Am. J. Soc. 60*:370-79, 1955.

Strodtbeck, F.L., and Mann, R.D. Sex role differentiation in jury deliberation. *Sociometry 19*:3-11, 1956.

Walter, W.G. Slow potential waves in the human brain associated with expectancy, attention and decision. *Arch. Psychiatr. Nervenkr. 206*:309-22, 1964.

Whittaker, J.O. Sex differences and susceptibility to interpersonal persuasion. *J. Soc. Psychol.* 66:91-92, 1965.
Whyte, W.F. *Street Corner Society*. University of Chicago Press, Chicago, 1943.
Zimmerman, D.H., and West, C. Sex roles, interruptions and silences in conversations. In: *Language and Sex: Difference and Dominance.* B. Thorne and N. Henley (Eds.), Newbury House, Rawley, MA, pp. 105-29, 1975.

Bibliographical Essay

In another half decade it may be possible to supply references that deal directly with sociophysiology or with the sociophysiology of hierarchies, and to provide presentations that are conceptually and empirically integrated. That is not possible now, but several sources can be recommended to those who wish to pursue aspects of the materials presented in this volume. For example, a grounding for the perspective of behavior in the context of evolution is provided by David Barash in *Sociobiology and Behavior* (Elsevier-North Holland, New York, 1977), and in *The Whispering Within* (Harper and Row, New York, 1979). Suggested also is Stephen Jay Gould's *The Panda's Thumb* (Norton and Company, New York, 1982).

In 1964, P.H. Leiderman and D. Shapiro edited *Psychobiological Approaches to Social Behavior* (Stanford University Press, Stanford, California). It is a forward-looking, interdisciplinary volume which contains information based on human experimental data that continues to be relevant to our understanding of small group behavior. "Physiological Sociology: Interface of Sociological and Biological Processes" (P.R. Barchas, *Annual Review of Sociology* 2:299-333, 1976) provides an earlier approach to understanding the socio-physiological processes involved in social behavior. *Psychophysiology: Human Behavior and Physiological Response* by J.L. Andreassi (Oxford University Press, New York, 1980) and *A Primer of Psychophysiology* by J. Hasset (W.H. Freeman and Company, San Francisco, 1978) provide thorough introductions to the measurement of physiological responses in relation to behavior. Each is recommended for the interested novice, each is comprehensible at the undergraduate level, and each provides sufficient information to permit a research program using electrophysiological methods to be launched.

Readers interested in a brief statement about behavioral mechanisms through which status relations are created and maintained should see "Status Organizing Processes" by J. Berger, S.J. Rosenholtz, and M. Zelditch, Jr. (*Annual Review of Sociology* 6:479-508, 1980). Those interested in the general application of processes of social exchange would do well to examine *Networks, Exchange, and Coercion: The Elementary Theory and Its Applications* (edited by D. Willer and B. Anderson, Elsevier-North Holland, New York, 1981). The conceptual framework which is presented rests on social relations as the basic building block from which the authors develop a general model of exhange. They report several studies that examine coercion, exploitation and domination in a variety of social contexts.

Readers who wish to explore the use of nonhuman primates to gain insight into social behavior may find relevance in ethologist Robert A. Hinde's 1983 publication, *Primate Social Relationships: An Integrated Approach* (Sinauer Associates, Inc., Sunderland, Mass.), as well as in his earlier works. The collection of papers edited by I. Hanen and E. Usdin, *Animal Models in Psychiatry* (Pergamon Press, New York, 1977), provides demonstrations of the imaginative ways a medical field closely related to social science has used animal models of behavior. *Stress, Health and the Social Environment* by J.P. Henry and P.M. Stephens (Springer-Verlag, New York, 1977) presents conceptually relevant material which has been worked out empirically in rodent colonies.

Further reading relevant to the interface of social behavior and pharmacologic action may be found in two articles bearing the same title, "Sociopharmacology." The first is an article by P. Barchas and J. Barchas in *Psychopharmacology: From Theory to Practice* (edited by J.D. Barchas, P.A. Berger, R.D. Ciaranello and G.R. Elliott, Oxford University Press, New York, 1977). The second article is by Michael T. McGuire and was published in *Annual Review of Pharmacological Toxicology* 22:643-61, 1982.

Toward an Ecology of Brain by Roger Walsh (S P Medical and Scientific Books, New York, 1981) is a provocative treatment of the effects of social and physical environments on the brain; while R.L. Klatsky's *Human Memory: Structure and Processes* (W.H. Freeman and Co., San Francisco, 1975) is a lucid treatment of basic cognitive processes, including attentional processes. Enoch Callaway's *Brain Electrical Potentials and Individual Psychological Differences* (Grune and Stratton, New York, 1975) provides a helpfully clear discussion of evoked potentials as phenomena produced by the brain and some of their promises for use in behavioral research.

Finally, while sociological approaches are missing, *Social Psychophysiology: A Sourcebook*, edited by J.T. Cacioppo and R.E. Petty (The Guilford Press, New York, 1983) brings together within one cover a wide range of contributions that will be valuable to anyone wanting to pursue an integrated and interdisciplinary approach to understanding human behavior.

Subject Index

Author Index

Contributors

Patricia R. Barchas is Assistant Professor of Sociology at Stanford University, California. Her research and publications center on the interface of social and physiological processes, especially as they occur in relation to small group structure and face-to-face interaction.

Robert Bolin is Associate Professor of Sociology at New Mexico State University. His publications include *Long-Term Family Recovery from Disaster* and his current research concerns the long-term effects of natural disasters on individuals and families. A book about the determinants of family response to environmental stresses such as disasters is forthcoming.

Susan B. Bolin is currently in the Department of Civil Engineering at New Mexico State University, where she is focusing on watershed problems in hydrology. Also a biologist, she has completed several studies on the ethology and ecology of birds and mammals.

Ivan D. Chase is Assistant Professor of Sociology and a member of the Graduate Program in Ecology and Evolution at the State University of

New York at Stony Brook. His research focuses on social inequality processes in humans and animals; he is continuing his studies of dominance hierarchies and has begun new investigations of the development of social relations in young children and the organization of work in cooperative groups.

M. Hamit Fisek is a Professor in the Social Science Department of Bogazici University in Istanbul, Turkey, where he teaches computer science and methodology. Also a specialist in small group processes, his publications in English include two coauthored books: *Expectation States Theory: A Theoretical Research Program* and *Status Characteristics and Social Interaction: An Expectation States Approach.*

Suzanne N. Haber is Assistant Professor of Anatomy at the University of Rochester, Rochester, New York. Her research has focused on the effects of drugs on primate social behavior and more recently on chemical circuitry of brain areas involved in emotional behavior.

William A. Harris is an experimental social psychologist at the College of the Virgin Islands, St. Thomas. His published work has focused on issues of power, legitimation, and the sociophysiology of status organizing processes.

William S. Jose II is a sociologist with particular interest in interpersonal processes. He is presently employed by Control Data Corporation in Minneapolis with responsibility for computer-based education.

Sally P. Mendoza is a comparative psychologist-ethologist who has specialized in the sociobiology of nonhuman primates. An experimentalist, her earlier work dealt with the impact of disrupted mother-infant bonds on physiology in monkeys. She is now pursuing her interests at the California Regional Primate Center, University of California, Davis.

Barbara A. Payne is a sociologist working at the Argonne National Laboratory in Illinois, where she is concerned with environmental impact studies.

Henry A. Walker is Assistant Professor of Sociology at Stanford University. His research and publications focus on issues of power, legitimation and status organizing processes at several levels of social organization.